T0123411

18
Forever

Suz Connors

BALBOA.
PRESS
A DIVISION OF HAY HOUSE

Balboa Press books may be ordered through booksellers or by contacting:

Balboa Press
A Division of Hay House
1663 Liberty Drive
Bloomington, IN 47403
www.balboapress.com
1 (877) 407-4847

Because of the dynamic nature of the Internet, any web addresses or links contained in this book may have changed since publication and may no longer be valid. The views expressed in this work are solely those of the author and do not necessarily reflect the views of the publisher, and the publisher hereby disclaims any responsibility for them.

The author of this book does not dispense medical advice or prescribe the use of any technique as a form of treatment for physical, emotional, or medical problems without the advice of a physician, either directly or indirectly. The intent of the author is only to offer information of a general nature to help you in your quest for emotional and spiritual well-being. In the event you use any of the information in this book for yourself, which is your constitutional right, the author and the publisher assume no responsibility for your actions.

Any people depicted in stock imagery provided by Getty Images are models, and such images are being used for illustrative purposes only. Certain stock imagery © Getty Images.

Print information available on the last page.

ISBN: 978-1-9822-0570-6 (sc)
ISBN: 978-1-9822-0571-3 (e)

Balboa Press rev. date: 07/03/2018

CONTENTS

Introduction vii
Wish

PART ONE

Chapter 1   Classic Lucas 1
Chapter 2   Family & Friends 8
Chapter 3   Babyhood & Toddlerdom 19
Chapter 4   Boytime 25
Chapter 5   Middle School – Tribulations & Triumphs 34
Chapter 6   Senior School Antics 46
Chapter 7   New Hope 62

PART TWO

Chapter 8   Diagnosis 67
Chapter 9   Treatment 72
Chapter 10   Hospital Life 78
Chapter 11   Side Effects 84
Chapter 12   Saving His Leg 87
Chapter 13   Chemo To ICU 90
Chapter 14   Tough Days 98
Chapter 15   18 Forever 107
Chapter 16   Lost Days 113

Chapter 17   Feelings 115

Chapter 18   Extraordinary 117

Afterword 121
        Change

Acknowledgements 123

About The Author 127

INTRODUCTION

Wish

Our precious son and Alisha's brother, Lucas, was taken from us on his 18th Birthday, 30/3/17. If there was anything in this world or beyond, I could wish for, it would be to bring my beautiful Lucas back. He was a very witty, intelligent and caring young man at the beginning of a fantastic and promising life. He was full of hope and ambition to make his mark in this world and was robbed of his dream, so tragically at the very last moment. The dream of being a Chemical Engineer embarking on his next chapter of life.

He was diagnosed in June 2016 with osteosarcoma, an aggressive and malignant bone tumour in his left knee. He underwent 3 months of high dose chemotherapy, then 'limb salvage surgery' to save his leg, (replacing bones with metal prosthetics), with more chemo that followed and eventually lead to multiple organ failures.

I think about him continuously day in and day out and that void will never be filled in my heart. If I chose to stay home and cry for the rest of my life it will not bring him back or change anything. So, what I *can* do, is turn my heavy bearing grief into something else, that I can share, as a tribute - a very brief, but a bright life story of Lucas.

I can only hope to be somewhat like my magnificent son and learn to appreciate and celebrate everything life brings me. And like Alisha said in her eulogy, I will live my life in dedication to his. What I *choose* to do now is move forward in my life and remember the amazing person he was and that makes me smile when I think of him.

PART ONE

CHAPTER ONE

Classic Lucas

There were so many things that made up Lucas. He was polite, well mannered, thoughtful, compassionate, well spoken, intelligent, protective, loyal, loving and funny. In later years, this combined with dedication, leadership skills, great work ethic and ability to speak to people at all levels made him the amazing person he was.

(The following are a collection of thoughts that reflect some of these qualities and are truly 'classic Lucas')

As a small boy Lucas, with Alisha following him, would love to be sprayed down with the garden hose by Les in the backyard, running around and screaming for more, Lucas usually being the loudest.

The backyard is also where he learnt to play cricket, play 'Donkey' (a ball game from my own childhood) and even learnt how to grow and look after fruit and vegetables - his prize tomatoes winning him a family pass to the zoo!

It is also the place where he would often take Max (Les' Eclectus parrot) out of his cage and onto the lawn. Max, would only let Lucas join him down on the lawn, while he enjoyed his time walking around freely, before Lucas returned him to his cage.

When Les and I were kids ourselves, we were both taken to Anglo Indian/Burmese family dances (our families' backgrounds), which were great fun for adults, but totally boring for kids. These were usually held as fundraisers for their respective associations. They always had daggy bands playing and it was a chance (for our parents mainly) to catch up with friends and relatives that they hadn't seen for a while. Following in our parents' footsteps, we took our own kids to these dances and they thought it was equally boring. But Lucas always got into the spirit of things and enjoyed himself in the process. He would make a point of dancing along with everyone else, but in particular next to his Aunty Beryl to Tina Turner's – 'Nutbush City Limits'. This always made her feel special and she referred to Lucas as her 'dancing partner'. He had a lot of respect for Aunty Beryl and would often sit and chat with her at family gatherings.

As Lucas had been fishing since he was little, a few years back when we were holidaying in Exmouth (north WA), Lucas a passionate fisherman by now, endured severe wind and sunburn to his lips, all for the thrill and excitement of fishing. The holiday house we were in had a jetty leading from the backyard onto the canals where the boat was moored. Regardless if the boat was going out that day or not, Lucas would be the first one out on the jetty fishing in the morning and the last one to come in at night. He was in his element catching fish after fish.

He also had an obsession with claw games, the machine games where you manoeuvre the claw to try and pick up a prize. He would win often on these games, but one time in particular he won a Go Pro camera, which he later used on the boat, to capture days out on the water catching fish.

Special occasions were always interesting. Like when putting up the Christmas tree in our house, it always began well, but usually ended with one or both kids storming off, usually Lucas first. They were excited to begin, but somehow this changed to arguments and they'd soon lose interest, leaving me to finish and clean up the mess they had made. On a couple of occasions for Christmas day, Lucas dressed up and played a fantastic Santa, giving out the presents to his younger cousins (Connors side). He even got the adults to sit on his lap and speak to Santa!

And at Easter time Lucas' generosity was amazing. At the end of the easter egg hunts, he would try to even out the number of eggs the kids collected, especially if he had more than anyone else. Usually coming away with a mountain of eggs himself, he would store his stash away in the pantry, but was always willing to share them with me – he understood my fixation with chocolate!

One thing he could not do, was 'a snack' for morning or afternoon tea, it always had to be a complete meal, his appetite was huge!

As we had taken our kids along with us to restaurants since they were babies, it was usual for them to dine out with us. Lucas was always well mannered, polite and confident in ordering and was happy to experience all different types of food.

He loved a good steak too, but I usually overcooked them, so *he* decided to start cooking them for Alisha and himself. He mastered the skill of medium rare perfection both on the BBQ and the cooktop.

A daily job both kids needed to do was empty the dishwasher. By no means was this hard work and they had the choice of either the top or bottom drawer (the top always had less in it). The deal was, whoever was there first would choose the drawer. Invariably they would forget to do it, so when I asked if it had been emptied, they would both run and try and get there before the other to 'win' the top drawer. This was another source of pushing, shoving and arguing, all in good sibling rivalry!

Lucas loved a good prank, especially involving his Nanna. She has a fear of lizards and creepy crawlies, so naturally Lucas used this to his advantage. There were many times a fake lizard, snake or spider would appear mysteriously in her house somewhere, each time getting a scream from Nanna and leaving him and his grandpa and cousins in fits of laughter.

Other times he would call his nanna or grandpa on the phone and pretend to be from an Indian call centre trying to sell them something, or even pretend to be friends from their church saying they were coming over.

Then there was the time Lucas had his grandpa in on the prank. Grandpa had asked him to help out by trimming the garden hedges and without Nanna realising, Lucas had swiped the tomato sauce bottle from the kitchen. He pretended to have been cut by the hedge-trimmer and was screaming and staggered inside with what Nanna thought was blood all over his hands. She started screaming at Grandpa for letting Lucas use the hedge-trimmer, until he showed her it was just sauce, while he and his grandpa were unashamedly laughing at his nanna's expense.

We have a lot of 'inside' jokes in our family.
And Lucas had these hilarious sayings, usually from TV shows or movies, that he recited 'in accent', which was so funny, like:
"Very nice, I quite like" – Borat
"No, no, no, no, no" – Family Guy
"George Costanza" - Seinfeld

Other classic Lucas sayings:
"Little boy" – referring to Alisha
"Unluckaay"
"Ohh Shiiit"
"Shhh, go to sleep, go to sleep"

"It's all good"
"What not"
"Ah, good job"

He would often order with an accent when we were at drive thru's of fast food outlets (I may or may not have started this!) Sometimes it was an American accent, sometimes Indian, sometimes Asian, sometimes he'd start in one accent and then finish in another.

Also while in the car, he would fall asleep, a habit he had since he was little. We could be driving for only five minutes and he would nod off. On our drive home from school most days, he would lay his passenger seat back and practically be lying down sleeping.

His friends were a major part of his life. "The Boys" and their banter were the bunch he was closest with, but he had many other friendship groups too. As he was invited to a lot of parties and had a keen interest in music, many times he was asked to organise the music playlists for the party and was proud to be asked this.

The day he turned 16 he got his L's (Learner's permit) straight after school had finished for the day. Not long after that he bought his car, a practically brand new black Holden Cruze, that he loved so much. He was so proud of it, as he had paid half of it from the money he earned at his part time job at Southside Pool Services (another thing he took pride in).

LUCAS WITH HIS CAR

One time after an oncology clinic hospital appointment, Lucas and I were walking back to the car and had passed some offices in the nearby business area. Lucas yelled out "Wooh!" and so did I in response, but he then just kept going with it. Only to realise there was an office worker standing out the front of a building watching him. Once he knew, he deliberately carried it on, continuing to yell out, pretending he was quite mad and running at the same time. I just went along with it while the office worker just kept curiously staring!

During a stay in hospital, a music teacher (oddly my old music teacher from high school), was on the ward with her ukulele and taught Lucas a few songs by his bedside. After this and the fact that Alisha had bought herself a guitar and was learning how to play, he was hooked. Alisha would sometimes let Lucas play hers, but only for a few minutes at a time, which was always another source of arguments.

On a day that Lucas was staying home to study while Alisha, Les and myself went out, Alisha just had this gut feeling and set her laptop up to video. Her instincts were right. She had caught Lucas on video coming into her room, finding her guitar and sitting down playing it while he had a decent chance! It was hilarious that he had been caught out and could not deny it. He bought his own guitar after that and taught himself how to play.

As big and crazy Lucas as he was, he remained kind hearted and loving. He would always make it a point to kiss and wish both Les and myself goodnight every night, something we will always treasure.

CHAPTER TWO

Family & Friends

Suz (Lucas' Mum)

I had the amazing privilege and honour of being the mother of this amazing young man. He and I shared many things and we had a close bond that will always unite us.

From the time Lucas was born I started a type of journal (for both kids) and wrote down all the positive significant things/events that happened in their lives. I was always diligent with this and wrote in it even when Lucas was in Year 12. I am so glad I did this, it brings me happy memories and has assisted me in writing this book too.

A stickler for tradition and sentiment, I always liked to celebrate the kids' 'half yearly' birthdays, up until they turned 13 (bit daggy for a teenager). It was a something they loved, while reminding us to celebrate that they had become half a year older and wiser. It was simply marked, by a candle in their piece of fruit, toast, or whatever breakfast was, while we sang 'happy half birthday'.

When the Tooth Fairy visited our home, she would always leave a few coins, a mini token, some scatter stars/love hearts all in a pouch, along with her note.

The Easter Bunny left paw prints leading up to the easter eggs on Easter Sunday.

And we always had to leave something out for Santa and his reindeer to eat. I am so grateful to have shared in the joy it brought to my kids, even when it left me with things to clean up!

As Lucas was growing up and achieving great things like lasting friendships, good manners, terrific grades and great work ethic, he was also developing a very funny sense of humour that I loved to encourage. He really understood the value of making people laugh and of not taking things too seriously.

As we had such similar wit, we enjoyed watching certain styles of movies and TV shows together, which made us look at each other and laugh hysterically.

When Lucas, Alisha and I watched shows together we'd often replay the funny scenes or lines over and over repeatedly, which became funnier each time - it was just something we just did!

LUCAS AND MYSELF WHILE OUR HOUSE WAS BEING BUILT

Les (Lucas' Dad)

Being the father of a bright boy, Les taught Lucas at a young age how to fix things. With this knowledge he knew how to work with his hands and understood how the mechanics of things worked or were put together.

LUCAS HELPING HIS DAD

But from the age of 4, Les started teaching him how to fish and this became his real love. Once Les had his first boat we would go out as a family fishing/boating together. By the time the next boat came along, Lucas was old enough to go out with his dad alone, which he absolutely loved, doing what he enjoyed and spending that one on one time together with his dad.

The other thing Lucas loved to do with Les and Alisha was watch action movies together. Some of the movies they loved to watch were:- DC & Marvel movies (his favourites), Star Wars, Lord of the Rings, the Fast & Furious, Rush Hour and Die Hard movies.

Lucas as a teenager of course loved to sleep, much to Les' horror of "Wasting the day!" He could sleep any time of the day or night.

From the time he was little he would always fall asleep in the car no matter how long the journey. When Les was driving, in order to wake him up when we neared home, Les would deliberately swerve the car when the road was deserted, so Lucas would bump his head on the window and we'd all get a good laugh, except a grumpy Lucas!

Alisha (Lucas' Sister)

Lucas adored his sister and was so proud and protective of her from a young age. They did everything together and were inseparable. When they were little, they were quite happy to sit squashed right next to each other on the same single sofa.

It was only as they grew into teenagers the arguments and fights started, like most siblings, but they still always looked out for each – they had a special bond.

As a young boy, Lucas spent so much time on his beloved Xbox and all Alisha wanted, was to be in the room with him when he was playing. For a long time, he just gave her a controller that wasn't even connected, so she would feel included, she didn't seem to notice that she wasn't actually playing. Then he finally taught her how to play, starting with a Shrek game and then later Call of Duty and GTA when they became older.

He helped her build numerous cubby houses and tents, but usually never helped her to pack things away!

WITH ALISHA IN HER CUBBY HOUSE

They would go out bike riding together, often it would end in Alisha coming back complaining that Lucas would be too far ahead of her, or took her out for too long.

They enjoyed watching certain movies and TV shows together. When they were little it was a countless repeat of the Shark Boy and Lava Girl movie and Around the Twist or Mortified on TV. Then as older kids, a favourite became White Chicks and Modern Family.

When we would sit at the table to have dinner, Alisha would somehow always end up resting her feet on Lucas, which he used to get so annoyed at and yell at her – such a weird habit, that she just automatically did and he put up with for years.

Some of the things Lucas did with and to her, in later years were strange, but hilarious, like putting her head under his t-shirt and pretending to suffocate her.

Other times he'd cover her mouth with his hand, pulling her backwards saying "Shhh, go to sleep, go to sleep".

He would call her "little boy" (affectionately of course) which she just went with.

And when making pancakes, they loved to squirt the dairy whip cream straight from the can into each other's mouths to full capacity too!

After his leg surgery and his leg muscle had weakened and shrunk, Alisha would tease him and call it his "Girly leg", which he thought was pretty funny.

Alisha would often go into his room to talk to him, but he would never let her sit on his bed. Agreeing, she would sit on his floor discussing things that happened at school, friends, music, whatever.

Daisy (Alisha's Dog)

Daisy (Alisha's miniature schnauzer) came to her a few days before Lucas' 15th birthday, which he was not happy about. Although we'd had a dog previously, Shima, whom Lucas liked, he was not keen on having another one. When the breeder brought the cute little puppy Daisy over, Lucas finally came out of his room and was annoyed that "it" was here. But he actually patted her, which is something he just didn't do. He even played in the backyard with Alisha and Daisy on that first day, which was very rare for him.

From then on, any time Daisy brushed past him and touched him in the slightest way, Lucas would have a shower, not wanting 'dog germs' on him. He eventually got it under control by just *washing* his leg/foot if she touched him instead of showering!

I took a photo once of Daisy with Lucas' shoe in her mouth and showed it to him in the hospital – he was so angry and I'm sure he would have thrown those shoes away if he was home. Occasionally he'd give her a biscuit or treat, being careful to never actually let her touch his hand, but I think he secretly liked her!

CONNORS FAMILY

Grandparents (Connors)

Lucas' grandfather on Les' side was Bunny Connors (Wilfred his actual name) and Lucas called him "Poppie." Bunny was so proud of his first grandchild and had a special bond with Lucas. When Lucas was little, Bunny proudly took him on his first train ride. As Bunny did not drive, he would catch a bus to our house (a fair distance), to come and spend time with Lucas when he could. He affectionately called Lucas "Champion" or "Champ" and everyone would know who Bunny was referring to. He always encouraged Lucas with his karate and came to so many of Lucas' karate gradings to support him. (Bunny sadly passed away when Lucas was 11).

Lucas' grandmother on Les' side is Faith Connors, whom Lucas called "Nannie". She always bragged about Lucas especially to her friends. She loved to take him to church when he was little and let him sit alongside her in the choir. From the time he was a toddler and Faith wanted to put him to sleep or just relax with him, she would gently scratch his back which Lucas loved and often asked her to do, it was a special thing only his Nannie could do. When he turned older she would often rely on Lucas to climb the mango tree in her backyard and pick the ripe mangoes for her, which he eagerly did.

Derek D'cruz

Derek is Les' cousin and Lucas always respectfully called him Uncle Derek and looked up to him. He would often talk to Lucas, giving him advice and encouragement in a range of different areas.

And he also generously loved to gift interesting or unusual things to Lucas that he found interesting.

DEREK AND LUCAS

WALLACE FAMILY

Grandparents (Wallace)

My dad is Ken Wallace and Lucas called him "Grandpa". He loved sport, so when Lucas was little would run around the backyard with him, or they'd play ball, cricket or soccer together. As Lucas matured his grandpa would always have some jobs lined up when we would visit, that he could help him with. Lucas and his grandpa developed an amusing banter and together often stirred his nanna with it.

My mum is Joan Wallace and was called "Nanna" by Lucas. She loved cooking and would always want to cook for Lucas and stuff him full of food. Everywhere Nanna went with Lucas, she would introduce him to everyone, much to his embarrassment when he was a pre-teen, as it was even to people like *local shop owners*. Both Nanna and Grandpa also taught the kids how to play Carroms (an Asian tabletop game). Often his grandpa and Lucas would pair up against Alisha and Nanna. They even bought Lucas his own Carrom board one year for his birthday.

Tash Palmer

Tash (Natasha Palmer) is my sister Christabelle's daughter and cousin to Lucas. Tash and Lucas have always been more like siblings than cousins. When they were young they used to fight so much, the same way siblings do, I would often have to separate them so there was some peace. When Lucas grew up they developed a strong 'cousins bond' and shared a special handshake when they saw one another.

LUCAS WITH HIS COUSIN TASH

LUCAS' FRIENDS

Declan De Waal

Declan was Lucas' first and longest time friend (since daycare), more like a brother. Even when they hadn't seen each other for a while because they went to different schools, it was like no time had passed when they caught up. They were great Xbox rivals and would play from morning till night if they could get away with it.

LUCAS WITH HIS GOOD FRIEND DECLAN

THE BOYS

This amazing group of boys that formed a deep and strong bond with their friend Lucas. James Holloway, Ricky Perdec, Peter Hill and Joseph Hobday.

THE BOYS

Peter Hill

Peter was Lucas' closest friend and had met in homeroom when they started high school in Year 7. These two would go on to work (more like goof around) on various extracurricular projects together and developed a strong friendship in the process.

Ricky Perdec

Ricky was in Lucas' Indonesian class with him, in Year 12 there being only eight of them. They had a common interest in rap music and in particular loved Eminem. Ricky, who performs rap and had taken on the rap name Psyfer, is now known as Wesley Black. He has written and recorded many songs, one of them dedicated to Lucas when he passed.

James Holloway

Lucas had known James since year one of primary school, but only really started hanging out in high school together. James is a great storyteller and Lucas enjoyed lots of banter with him.

Joseph Hobday

Joseph was in many of Lucas' classes in high school and led to a friendship spurred on by friendly rivalry and banter.

(These chapters are written in a chronological sequence of events or experiences as they happened over time)

CHAPTER THREE

Babyhood & Toddlerdom

After being blissfully married for 6 years, Les and I thought maybe we could slow down our partying and start a family. 9 months later Lucas Anthony Connors, this amazing little bundle of squishiness was born and was one of the most thrilling days of our lives!

On the day I was in labour, our parents were so excited, that all four of them met at the hospital and came in to the birthing suite to be with us. Meanwhile, I was having contractions and trying to smile politely at them, until it all became too much and Les had to ask them to leave (only after they'd finished our food, that we weren't eating!) Being the first grandchild in the Connors family and the first grandson on the Wallace side, everyone was incredibly happy for us.

PROUD GRANDPARENTS, JOAN, KEN (HOLDING LUCAS), FAITH AND BUNNY (WITH TASH)

My nickname for Lucas was Bouge (*Boo-d-j*), because I would sit him on my lap as a baby and bounce him up and down and say "a bouge, a bouge, a bouge", so it just stuck.

We are lucky that he did not in fact *get* stuck in the various things we placed him in, all to get an awesome photo! He was placed in pots, drawers, laundry baskets, all sorts of crazy spots.

From a baby, his enormous ear to ear smile left you with that warm fuzzy feeling in your heart of such love for this sweet little boy. He was always smiling and so willing to please, a charming characteristic he grew up with also. His cheeky but loveable nature endeared him to everyone that he came across.

LUCAS AS A TODDLER WITH HIS GORGEOUS SMILE

But at home this little terror would try and get into our kitchen cupboards and drawers constantly. I remember having to buy those special baby locks that are fitted to cupboard doors and safety plugs for the power points. I also became inventive, using one of my belts to secure the handles on our kitchen drawers together. Those little fingers just wanted to touch and investigate everything.

Sometime in early 'babyhood' when he had learned to climb, Lucas (when we weren't looking) thought he would climb our solid, tall wooden cabinet, which held our 'pre-plasma' bulky TV. As he pulled himself up by gripping onto the TV, it came away from the cabinet and crashing towards the ground, as did he. It dangled precariously by it's cord - still thankfully plugged into the power point on the wall and missed crushing him by mere centimetres!

Around 6 months old he and I took our first plane flight together to Adelaide, to visit my pregnant sister Michelle and her husband Duncan who were living there at the time. Apart from persistently pulling his shoes and socks off at the airport before we left, much to my mum's horror, the rest of the trip was relatively smooth sailing considering he was so little.

His first Christmas was interesting, as being so little he of course didn't understand what all the fuss was about. I remember when at my parents' home, opening all the gifts he had been spoilt with, he just wanted to play with his cousin, my niece Tash (who was about 7 at the time) and excitedly scrunched up and threw around the Christmas wrapping paper. That was all it was about for him.

He began walking at 9+1/2 months which was very exciting for Les and myself, but of course a lot more work constantly watching him, a lot earlier than we had expected.

We had some pot plants outside our backyard doors that were topped with pea gravel. Every time Lucas went outside, the gravel was like a magnet that he was drawn to. He had to pick up handfuls of it and throw it around and laugh when he had done this too - little buggar!

One time when we were in the backyard, before we could stop him, he had taken Les' hammer and hit our faithful Sharpei dog Shima on her back with it. All she did was growl at him, poor thing.

He would often pull things apart as if trying to see how they worked and even try to put them back together. This was when Les started to teach him small 'fix it' things and he started sucking the information up like a sponge. We bought him a 'Bob the Builder' toy tool belt and helmet especially so he could be 'daddy's helper'.

Because he was literally on the move now, of course he did not like to be in his stroller much. I vividly remember when I met my good friend Vanessa at an outdoor cafe in Kings Park, how he quite casually got up out of his stroller and suddenly started running toward the road. I have never moved so fast. I jumped the roped off cafe area and bolted after him, grabbing him before he could get to the road, thank goodness!

Then there was the time I had given him his evening bath and changed him into his pyjamas. I found him soon after in the bath tub, pyjamas and all, playing happily with that big smile of his across his face. I always remembered to drain the bath tub immediately after that little incident.

Around his first birthday my maternity leave came to an end and I had returned to work part time. I moved my work location within Western Power so I could be closer to home for Lucas. After trying several different daycare centres, I finally found the one I was most happy with, which was also close to home. This is where Lucas met his first buddy Declan. These two mischievous but adorable little boys played so well together and eventually went on to school together.

It was not long after he had turned 2 that Lucas told his first lie! I had seen him mark a wall at home with an inked stamp. When Les asked him if he had done it, he quite definitively said "No"!

This was about the time he could say his own name as "Lucas Connors", a big improvement on "Doodas"

He also called a helicopter a "hapicockter"

An orange an "oninge"

And our all-time favourite - "Look daddy, a fuck!"

By the time he was 2+1/2 he had flown with me to Geraldton and back, this time to see his dad who was working there at the time.

When he turned 3 we had the best news of all to give him, that he was going to have a new brother or sister. Adamant from the start, he said he only wanted a baby "thister".

During this pregnancy of mine, Lucas had picked up chicken pox from daycare and it was an almost impossible feat for me as a heavily pregnant mother to keep a 3year old from itching and scratching. I had to be vaccinated against chicken pox too, to protect the baby, unfortunately I still caught it, so now I had spots all over my huge pregnant tummy as well.

Lucas was 3+1/2 when Alisha was born and was so proud of his new baby "thister". It was Lucas who chose Alisha's middle name of Louise or as he called her "Aweez". He had finished at daycare now, as Les and I had made the decision that I would resign from work. We were fortunate that Les' career afforded me the opportunity of being home with the two of them, of which I'm so appreciative.

He started kindergarten just prior to turning 4 and he and Declan were in the same class. They were still best friends and enjoyed being at school together. At the end of Pre-Primary though they both left this school and went to different schools but remained playmates.

We had a 4th birthday party for Lucas in our backyard with his cousins, daycare and school friends and had Bananas the Clown perform, who the 4year olds loved.

This was around the time Les who had always loved fishing since *he* was a child, decided to take Lucas fishing with him. Lucas instantly loved it too and it was the beginning of many fishing trips together.

CHAPTER FOUR

Boytime

When he was a little boy Lucas would love nothing better after school than to play with his then baby sister Alisha. As they both grew, he was fiercely protective of her and would defend her around his cousins and friends alike.

PLAYTIME WITH ALISHA IN THE INFLATABLE POOL

He loved doing all sorts of crazy brother-sister things with her. I recall countless cubby houses being built from sheets, cushions and couches.

One of the games Lucas, Alisha and I played every day without fail was 'spaceships', a game we had devised together, that involved beanbags, aliens, pretend aliens guns and a lot of imagination.

As much as he enjoyed playing with his sister and mum, going to the park, or kicking the ball in the backyard, he of course loved boytime too.

Les would often take him fishing on his boat or even fishing from the jetty or the rocks. This was Lucas' real passion, he loved the thrill of trying to catch a fish (or a crab on the rocks when he was tired of fishing).

He loved all things Spiderman too. He would dress up in his costume and climb up between the two walls in our kitchen and just hang there pretending to be Spiderman. Then he would run around the house holding out his hand pretending to spray a web and saying "Psssssttt, I'll put you in my web."

The Wiggles featured on our TV screen so much, that when I was doing mundane jobs like vacuuming, I had their songs playing over in my head! Lucas was so excited when he was taken to see The Wiggles and Hi 5 perform live in concert.

He was obsessed with his first Xbox that Santa had brought him when he was in Kindy. Lucas would become so angry and worked up when he had lost a game, but soon became very fast and precise with his coordination, *that* I must credit Xbox with. However, because he was so keen to play, it also became a great source of punishment when he misbehaved and was not allowed to play on it. Most nights after we had tucked him into his bed, Les and I would have so much fun sneakily playing Xbox together.

One thing I had taught him soon after Alisha was born and when we were at the shops, was that he needed to either hold onto Alisha's pram or the shopping trolley, so he would be safe. He did this so well, to the point, that as he got a little older I had to tell him to walk alongside it instead of holding onto it, as he was slowing me down too much!

As he grew, Les introduced him to Star Wars movies and he absolutely loved them, watching these movies over and over and over!

My Brother-in-law Darren is a fire fighter and took Lucas on his firetruck and for a look around the station when he was 3. Then again for his 5th birthday, this time with Declan and Tash. He was lucky enough to do this again with Alisha and Darren's son Jordy. This time I joined them too on a ride in the firetruck, with sirens blaring intermittently, the kids thought this was fantastic. Darren also helped Lucas to use the fire hose in the fire station which Lucas was pretty excited about.

Another time, Les had arranged one of his workers to take Lucas up in a 'boom lift', another awesome experience for a little boy, maybe all this is where his enthusiasm for scary/dangerous rides came from!

He also had a mania for Timezone (an amusement arcade). The amount of times Lucas and Alisha together had dragged us there, I've lost count! The other place they always pleaded with us to go was Scitech (a science discovery centre), but they would be bored after about 15 minutes and we wondered why we were there in the first place!

On our first trip to Penang with the kids, we visited the Penang Butterfly Park, where Lucas spent most of the time trying to catch the butterflies in their enclosures. When we returned to our hotel later, I discovered pieces of squashed butterflies in the pockets of his shorts.

Penang was also where he had learned his daredevil jetskiing skills with Les. He also found it hilarious that Alisha had strangely fallen asleep whilst on the jetski with me (that is pretty odd!)

Lucas was usually willing to play anything with Alisha. I remember one time, Lucas even dressing Alisha up in his clothes so she was a mini Lucas. Then she dressed him in one of her fairy dresses complete with head-dress and we were calling him "Lucasina".

His cheekiness often led him to being up to some sort of mischief at home or around family. Like when we rented a house in Kardinya that was built on a steep, sloping street. The incline of the street made it easy for him to climb the limestone wall on one side of the house, from there leap onto the roof (Spiderman style) and then jump off it and land on the grass below, till I finally managed to stop him.

Years before, we had bought him a plastic car that he could drive around in which he loved. By now he was an expert at manoeuvring around in it. He used to take turns with Alisha and roll down the backyard of the Kardinya house deliberately crashing into the limestone retaining wall at the bottom of the slope!

As we had moved houses, Lucas moved primary schools too, from Canning Vale Catholic (now known as St Emilie's), to Yidarra Catholic Primary where he started Year 1. It was an interesting transition for him, he was excited to start there, but I think he always felt a little left out, with many of the kids having forged friendships there since Kindy.

We went on a camping trip with The Palmers to Peaceful Bay (south WA). The kids loved this and Lucas was loving being in amongst nature. He fished, caught frogs, explored and enjoyed being with Tash and Alisha.

Around the age of 8 he encountered bullying as is common in many schools. As he was well behaved and had a placid nature it unfortunately made him an easy target for bullies. One such time, a smaller made boy, in the same year group, was continually picking on

Lucas. It was hard as a parent to know whether to intervene or not, as we were trying to build resilience in our kids.

The final straw came when Les had decided, after Lucas explained who the bully in question was and that he was physically smaller than Lucas, something needed to be done. He enrolled Lucas in karate to learn self-defence, discipline and build his confidence whilst doing so.

And that is exactly what it did. He became confident fairly quickly, discipline he had never had a problem with and the art of self-defence was being learned. He won a triple samurai sword for his 'kata' (routine) in his first karate tournament against older opponents. This was probably around the time he pleaded with me to stop calling him "Bouge" in public!

A classmate whose family we were friendly with, had told Lucas that she liked him around this time too. Their friendship was never the same after that – probably to her disappointment. But Lucas was adamant he did not want any 'girl germs'!

He still enjoyed his primary years and went to and had many parties with friends. Some of these kids remained friends with him well into high school - James, Brendon, Desiree, Ciara and India to name a few.

His primary teachers thought he was a lovely boy with the term "Model student" being used a number of times over the years. His Year 4 teacher called him the "Moral compass of the class" and used him to gauge when things were getting out of control in the classroom.

He had become a good reader but was not too interested in reading. In an effort to encourage him I bought him 'Captain Underpants' books which he loved - better *some* reading than none. However, when the time came for an interview with his prospective future high school and he was asked what books he liked to read, guess what his answer was? Well at least they knew we had not prepped him for his interview!

Year 4 was a big year, in that the Year 4 kids were now included in the school swimming carnival. Even though Lucas was a strong swimmer, he wanted to practice in preparation for the carnival. We decided to go to Beatty Park Leisure Centre and make a fun family day of it and he would be able to practice there too. Being a beautiful day, we used the outdoor pool. The centre had set up a large inflatable obstacle course which the kids had fun playing on, until suddenly Lucas was stung on his posterior by a wasp! That was it, the fun was over and we headed straight to the chemist for some antihistamine relief. We still call it "Wasp park" today and have a chuckle when we drive past it. The short lived practice session paid off though, as he came first in his freestyle race and second in backstroke, at his first swimming carnival!

His caring and empathetic nature was becoming more evident. He decided that he wanted to help raise money and awareness of kids with leukaemia. He sought permission from his school and had his hair shaved as part of the World's Greatest Shave fundraising initiative.

At karate he had won another samurai sword for 'Most Dedicated Student' and we were all so proud. As Alisha had also begun karate, they would often train together, so when Alisha later followed in his footsteps and won this award too he was thrilled and so proud of her. He also collected a number of medals from various karate tournaments over the years.

The four of us went to Busselton (south of Perth) for a mini holiday before he began his final primary school year. This was a great break for all of us, with lots of fishing, swimming and games being played. The kids loved being allowed to move around the holiday park together, as Lucas was the protective and sensible older brother.

Year 6 had started well for him and as his confidence grew, so did *he*. But still, the bully from a few years earlier, (who had remained small), bugged him from time to time. One time when he picked on him, Lucas simply picked him up and moved him out of the way!

Finally, Lucas' patience had run out with him and on the next bullying occasion laid three punches into him. Les was so proud that Lucas had finally stood up for himself and to this bully (and quietly fist pumped the air!) Unfortunately, the school was not so impressed and resulted in a 'behaviour plan' being given to him. Needless to say, that bully never bothered him again.

He went on to win more races in his school swimming carnivals.

He was chosen for the interschool League Tag team and played in the T20 cricket carnival.

In Year 6 he was selected to represent the school alongside the Principal, at the Performing Arts Festival opening ceremony mass for catholic schools, held at St Mary's Cathedral.

And was a member of the school choir at the Performing Arts Festival.

He also became an altar server at the school parish.

Being involved in his school life meant so much to him at his young age.

The other thing that had happened was that two *more* girls had told him that they liked him - something he surprisingly shared with us!

Although we had a dog – Shima, Lucas was never a real animal lover. This changed somewhat when Les brought home a baby Max (his Australian Eclectus Parrot). After spoon feeding him, he soon grew and so did his strong beak and claws and his ability to speak, which was amazing. Lucas spent a lot of time teaching him, as did Les, with the result they were the only ones who could hold him. Lucas helped Les to take him out of his cage, clip his wings, shower him and play with him and became used to the scratches on his arms from Max's sharp claws.

Not long after both Lucas and Alisha were given Weiro's/ Cockatiel's by their Poppie and they named them Jack & Pinky. It was all cute at first, but eventually these birds were given back to their Poppie as they emitted an odour, that particularly Lucas could no longer stand.

During winter, Lucas went on his first fishing trip away to Shark Bay with Les and *his* friend Ron who made this long trip annually towing the boat. The trip soon became memorable, but not in the way he would have liked, as they neither did much fishing *or* boating. They were stranded on the water on the first day out there, as there was a fuel problem on the boat. Les was vigilant about every aspect of his boat and was frustrated with this. Regrettably they had to be towed back to shore by brand new, first time used, rescue boat – 'Tamala Rose'. The boat took days to be fixed by mechanics and then they finally headed back to Perth fishless, but happy enough.

Later in the year, a couple of the other trouble makers from his year group at school, decided to bully Lucas again. But according to Lucas this time they had gone too far. They had made derogatory comments about myself to him. When I picked him up from school he was clearly upset, I had to pry it out of him, while we were still in the school carpark. It was not easy for him and he was reluctant to tell me, but I could not tolerate any more bullying. I went straight to his teacher's classroom and the trouble makers were reprimanded the next day thankfully.

Graduation from primary school was finally here for him. He was really happy and looking forward to going to high school!

Just after graduation we had moved into our new home in Piara Waters. The kids were happy being in their new rooms and were enjoying swimming in their own pool.

We moved in a few days before Christmas. Les and my Brother-in-law Alex were still loading trailer loads of 'man cave stuff' to bring over to the new place. The kids and I were in the pool, when my sister Christabelle turned up to come along with us to the big Christmas Eve outdoor mass at the school parish, where Lucas was to do a reading. We had gotten carried away with swimming and not realised the time, jumped out of the pool (and our bathers) and made a mad dash to mass, luckily on time!

CHAPTER FIVE

Middle School – Tribulations & Triumphs

February 2011 and Lucas had matured into an intelligent, compassionate and humorous young boy. He finally started high school at Corpus Christi College and was happy to be there. He had begun the year positively and was filled with enthusiasm.

He made a whole new circle of friends at school and 'The Boys' (group of friends) were formed, comprising Peter, Ricky, Joseph, and James (from Yidarra). The extended group included Tom, Luke, Matt, Lachlan and a few others. These boys were like minded, competitive in a friendly way, but always spurred each other on and importantly had each other's backs. As a parent, I could have not asked for a better group for my son.

The Year 7 middle school group was fortunate to have an inspirational teacher in Lennon Rego. Lennon played a part in The Boys' friendship formation as he knew some of them well through his classes and grouped them together to work in teams.

Lennon had set one of Lucas' classes' an assignment which involved each group staying over someone's house and filming various skits etc. We lived across from a park which Lucas' group needed for the skit, so our home was chosen by the group. Some of The Boys were part of this and it was great to see their sense of fun and camaraderie coming out in the group work.

During that first middle school year, the teachers would often email parents to give them feedback about their child's progress. Lennon had emailed us that Lucas was doing well, but perhaps could be a little more organised. Lucas took this to heart and revised his whole schoolwork ethic. He colour-coded his different study notebooks, set up his room and printer to work more efficiently and from then started to really apply himself at school.

This initial prompt from Lennon helped Lucas then go on to receive many Letters of Commendation for Science, Maths, Humanities and Indonesian.

He played extracurricular cricket for Corpus, with soccer to follow later in the year. He also altar served at the school's Grandparents Day mass, which my parents were of course thrilled about. He was really enjoying being part of the school community.

In the June school holidays, we flew to Broome (north WA) for some sun, fishing and relaxation. Lucas experienced his first fishing charter with Les, which was a big thrill for him and pretty successful too.

While we were in Broome, we visited the Malcolm Douglas Crocodile Park, along with Les' cousin Nicole and her daughter Sienna who live in Broome. When it came time for the park attendants to bring out the baby crocodiles for members of the audience to hold, Lucas and Alisha both volunteered. One at a time they were handed (half a metre long), baby crocodiles and both of them, dropped the poor things! As the crocs scurried away, the unimpressed park attendants were running around trying to catch them. Unbelievably, they had both done this at separate times, in plain sight for everyone to see!

Back in Perth, Year 7 also saw Lucas' first girlfriend appear. Alisha naturally teased Lucas about her and he would cringe. I had never actually managed to catch a glimpse of her during school pickup. Alisha would always remark when she had spotted her, but with a carpark full of kids in the same uniform, it was an impossible task for me to spot the right girl as I was driving through. Whilst on a visit to Hong Kong Lucas had brought a gift back for her, but not long after that she broke up with him. We had a 'commiserations' afternoon tea at Hungry Jacks that day to help his broken heart get through.

Hong Kong was one of our great trips. With the kids a little bit older now we were able to do a lot more. Les had worked in Hong Kong in 1992 and we were able to show the kids where he had lived, which was great as it was such a different style of living to what they knew of in Perth. They were fascinated by the hustle and bustle of Hong Kong and Lucas especially with all the gadgets and tech galore (his nickname was 'Gadget Boy'). But the favourite by far was Disneyland which we all enjoyed, until Les made us leave during the fireworks at night - who does that?

When he was not at school, Lucas enjoyed his fishing, Xbox, riding his bike around the neighbourhood and all things boyish. His awesome sense of humour was starting to emerge now. At that time, he enjoyed watching Bear Grylls (the adventurer) on TV. I have an awesome video of Lucas in a bushy area of a park, doing a hilarious skit where he is imitating Bear 'surviving in nature'.

He had become a reliable helper to Les when it came to handiwork and I gladly delegated my official 'TA' (Trade Assistant) title over to him.

He still enjoyed hanging out with his (Wallace side) cousins too, who were all around the same ages (Tash being the oldest). Alisha had begged him to go trick or treating for Halloween with Issey & Ruby, which he did, dressed up as a demon and wholly embracing the lolly side of things.

The other cousins (Connors side) were still quite little, but Lucas loved playing and running around in his Nannie's backyard with them.

With the end of the first year of high school, came Lucas' nomination of Corpus' St Mary of the Cross Award. This award recognised a student's outstanding all-round contribution to college life. We were thrilled when he had been nominated by the teachers. I received a phone-call from a very excited Lennon, to tell me Lucas had been chosen as the recipient of this award and then he handed the phone to an equally excited Lucas. He received this prestigious award and certificate at the final assembly for the year.

He was also chosen as a Student Leader for his house Merici, (for the following year) for which he also received a house leadership badge. The awards ceremony that day was a proud moment for us all.

2012 - YEAR 8

We began 2012 with an extremely long drive to Exmouth (1260 km north of Perth) towing Les' boat with my parents and The Palmers accompanying us. To break up the long journey we stayed overnight in Denham, Shark Bay.

Whilst there, we drove to Monkey Mia, where the dolphins come to shore to swim and feed. Lucas and Alisha were chosen from the crowd to feed the dolphins which was an amazing experience for them and thrilling too for all of us.

We enjoyed Exmouth (when we finally got there), relaxing, fishing, boating and the lovely food. But we were stuck there for longer than anticipated due to bushfires blocking off the only road from Exmouth back to Perth in the searing summer heat.

The roads were finally re-opened and we could at last make our way back to Perth. The four of us stopped overnight in Kalbarri to break up the drive home.

We had taken a car trip to Nature's Window (a rock formation on a clifftop, the perfect photo opportunity). The deep valley walk that led to Nature's Window was an extremely hot one, although the distance to Nature's Window did not seem that far and we were eager to take some awesome photo's.

At Nature's Window, Kalbarri, WA

After we had spent our time taking in the views and were satisfied with the pictures, we made our way back through the valley again, keen to get out of the blazing sun. The heat was so intense now, that it made the same distance back to the car, feel endless. We were all struggling to walk, our energy drained away and made worse by the depletion of our supplies of water. Les and I both held the kid's hands, dragging them along behind us and frequently stopping, from sheer exhaustion and probably heat stroke, on the seemingly infinite stairs leading back to the car. It was only then that we saw the warning sign that the valley could reach temperatures of around 50 degrees Celsius during summer!

We staggered back into the car, after what felt like an eternity, the air conditioner blasting and all of us desperate for a drink. We stopped at a service station on the way back to town for drinks and fuel.

When we had cooled down and quenched our thirsts, trying not to be deterred from our experience, we realised something more leisurely was now necessary. We decided on the Kalbarri Bird Park and headed off, joking that at least we were a little better prepared this time.

As we drove out of town the car began to splutter and jerk, until it finally came to an abrupt stop. That's when Les realised he had filled his 4WD with petrol instead of diesel, the result of heatstroke no doubt. We managed to move the car a little further towards town until it failed altogether. Leaving Alisha and myself to walk back into town, while Les and Lucas remained behind to wait for someone to tow the car. The existing fuel had to be dumped and the car refilled with diesel this time!

Lucas started off Year 8 well and took great pride in his Student Leadership role. His duties as an altar boy being recognised again, this time on the oval at the commencement of the new school year community mass.

For his 13th birthday he simply enjoyed a day at Adventure World (water amusement park). A day of fun and just being kids, spent with his friends, Alisha, Les and myself. We also celebrated the arrival of his teenage years with our families on another day.

In the July school holidays we travelled to Singapore. The kids loved Universal Studios and we had bought them 'fast track passes' so they could enjoy their 'multiple' rides on each attraction without having to queue for them.

A weird thing we did as a family while we were there was to have a fish spa pedicure. This is where tiny fish eat the dead skin from your feet. An oddly ticklish experience that we had to try, even though Lucas did not think much of the idea, he still joined in with us.

Every spring season, we would visit Araluen Botanical Park in the Perth hills, to take in the beautiful blooms. We went as a family when possible, (but mainly for my benefit) although Lucas understandably was no longer keen to go. That year Les was not able to make it due to work, but Lucas, still wanting me to be able to see it, came along with Alisha, their scooters in tow and ended up having a fun time there.

Les' workshop stored the equipment that was used on various job sites. Les had bought a forklift to move the equipment around easily and Lucas was eager to use it. With a quick lesson from Les on how to drive it, Lucas was doing laps with it in the workshop carpark.

Later that year Les was working on a job in Exmouth and flew Lucas there to meet him and of course go on a fishing charter. Alisha and I joined them soon after, for a mini getaway.

Not being much of an art enthusiast, Lucas was pretty happy when his 'Red Dog' clay sculpture was included in the school art exhibition that year. Red Dog sits proudly on the TV cabinet in our home.

During the October school holidays we visited Phuket, with Les' mum Faith and his sister Belinda and her family. The kids had a great time especially in the pools together. We enjoyed ourselves and experienced both an elephant ride and an ox pulled bulla cart ride, whilst on a tour in the hills.

When we went for a stroll down Bangla Road in Patong where the 'ladyboys' were, Lucas really freaked out. He was particularly disturbed when we were greeted by numerous ladyboys. One in particular who had struck up a conversation with us asked Les to give her a kiss on her lips. Les declined, though humoured her and gave her a quick peck on the cheek. I have never seen Lucas in such shock and disbelief, he was stunned by it.

Back in Perth, my Brother-in-law Pete had bought a new motorbike. He took Lucas for a ride around their suburb on it. Lucas was pretty happy with himself when he came back, as he was the only one of the cousins (Connors side) that was old enough to go on the ride.

We enjoyed holidaying a fair bit that year. When another successful year of school was finished, the four of us headed to Bunker Bay (south of Perth). We stayed at the beautiful Bunker Bay Resort. The kids enjoyed lots of swimming and being surrounded by mother nature for a change.

2013 - YEAR 9

The bizarre year of teenage attitude and moodiness that is Year 9 had started fairly calmly. The addition of braces made Lucas feel somewhat awkward, but he got over it quickly, as he soon realised how many other kids had them too. He was always fairly slack with looking after his braces properly, but somehow seemed to get raving reviews from his Orthodontist, much to Alisha's annoyance when she got her own braces.

Handball was a popular game among The Boys during lunch breaks at school. There was an incident when another boy randomly stole their ball and tried to start a physical fight with Lucas, after refusing to return the ball to them. Lucas blocked this boy's moves and the boy subsequently fell into the nearby bushes.

Because he had been humiliated in front of his peers he 'dobbed' Lucas in to a teacher on duty and he was subsequently given an 'in school detention' for this. When we found out what had happened we were happy that Lucas had stood up to the bully, but were furious that the detention was an 'in school' one. It basically meant he had to miss out on classes for a whole day - clearly a waste of a school day, even Lucas agreed. Les spoke to the Deputy Principal, the detention time was changed and the Deputy even agreed that it was a ridiculous punishment to be given. Luckily for that boy, Lucas had demonstrated massive restraint, as he could have put his karate skills to use and done some real damage to him not just embarrassment.

His 14th birthday was shared by many of his friends with a party in our home. Lucas had made a lot of good friends in his year group, girls as well as boys, so there was quite a large number of kids at his party. I remember being shocked, as this was the first time Les and I noticed the way the girls dressed, (so sophisticated, like they were going clubbing), while the boys just wore their trademark t-shirts and shorts/jeans. We even had to tell Lucas before his own party to dress up a little more, so he put a shirt over the top of his t-shirt, about as stylish as a 14year old boy gets! The party went well except for all the lollies we found later thrown in the swimming pool.

Not long after this, we headed up to Denham, Shark Bay and celebrated his actual birthday there. Being with some family friends and just being 14, he cringed when we all sang Happy Birthday to him in the restaurant.

Lucas loved his fishing and boating more than anything else (Xbox comes a close second!) Les had begun teaching him how to drive the boat and he was very confident with this. Up until that point we had either gone out on the boat as a family, or Les and Lucas had taken friends out fishing. But as his boating certainty and abilities had grown, he was now ready to out go out 'deep sea' fishing, just the two of them, something they both loved.

DRIVING THE BOAT

Even though he was old enough to drive the boat, he was not too grown up to still do some things with his younger sister. I took them ice-skating and was proud to see him holding Alisha's hand and talking her through how to ice skate.

Alisha's favourite thing to do at the time was to have picnics with us, even if it was only in the backyard. Lucas would usually come along for a few minutes, just long enough to eat most of the food!

During June-July he went on a study tour of Indonesia with some students and teachers from school. He visited Yogyakarta where he attended classes at the university and Surabaya where he stayed with his host family and went to school.

We had agreed before he left Perth that he needed to be in contact with us daily, but being 14 meant that it was not cool and this was *conveniently* forgotten. Les and I were in a constant state of worry at the lack of contact supposedly due to poor internet or not enough time on Lucas' side. Les had become so worked up by this that he nearly jumped on a plane and dragged Lucas back to Perth, until I talked him out of it. Not quite the experience we were hoping he would have, but still, he had seen another country without his parents now. To his good fortune he ended up getting the Indonesian award at school that term!

Over the course of a year, the Year 9 students had to create their Personal Project. This involved something the student was passionate about that they could make/do/perform etc and compile a report detailing the process and their outcome. The teacher looking after the project was Lennon Rego. At that stage Lucas had wanted to become an architect so his project was to plan and create a model of his dream house.

I nervously watched him use the electric saw at home to cut his wood, Les quite confident that he had taught him well. It was a brilliant piece of work and he was so proud of it. His report - 'My Dream House' was very well written and detailed. So well in fact, that Lennon used it as an example of an 'excellent report' - which is still used at school today for current Year 9 personal projects. Lucas was very proud of his efforts and was rewarded for it by receiving a High Distinction by Lennon for his project on exhibition night.

Meanwhile, during a busy school year, Les had taken Lucas out on some deserted roads near our home, to drive for the first time. He was really excited by this and I am sure would have bragged about it to The Boys, as they were all still so young.

The end of year meant it was middle school graduation time. Their graduation ceremony was held at the function centre – 'Tompkins on Swan'. Les along with a lot of other parents were proudly taking group photos of the kids and their friends while everyone was arriving, but Les decided to take it a bit further. When the kids all headed inside the function centre, so did he, taking photos of The Boys at their table, along with other friends of Lucas', much to his great embarrassment. It was amusing to see from the pictures, that at this awkward teenage stage, the girls and boys still seemed to sit separately, but enjoyed the atmosphere of their combined company.

As school finished for the kids, Lucas had one more thing to achieve that year, he would attempt his Junior Black Belt in Karate. He had been training hard for it, during what was a really busy year for him. Although he had obviously done numerous karate gradings before, this was the one he wanted the most and was fairly nervous beforehand.

We watched proudly as he executed many different kata's (routines) with strength and accuracy. But I winced watching the continuous kumite (sparring) bouts, with many different challengers specifically chosen to spar with him, so he could demonstrate his skill and endurance at a high level. He was completely shattered at the end of it, but he had done it. He was awarded one of the first Junior Black Belts in his club!

We left for Kota Kinabalu in high spirits the next day for our Christmas holiday break. This holiday the kids really bonded again which was awesome. We had a fantastic Christmas day itself, going on a wild banana boat ride. Lucas and I both managed to fall off and he was freaking me out about sharks being in the water – typical! They went jet skiing too, something they loved to do. This was one of the most fun overseas holidays we have had.

CHAPTER SIX

Senior School Antics

We started the year by once again heading up to Denham, Shark Bay this time with Les' sister Jacqui & her family accompanying us. The kids had a ball hanging out together and they loved their fishing sessions with Lucas spurring them on. We took them to Monkey Mia and this time Jaida & Liam were chosen to feed the dolphins.

When they headed back to Perth, the four of us stayed on for an extra day together. While we were sitting on the balcony of our chalet Lucas and Alisha began throwing food scraps into the air and watching the seagulls catching them. Suddenly there were flocks of them swarming around the rooftop in a raucous food fighting frenzy, the kids laughing, throwing more and more deliberately.

Back in Perth Lucas thought it was time to start shaving. After a quick check with Les, who teased him that he only had some "bumfluff", he began and was feeling quite proud and gave him something to boast about.

Still on holidays, I took the kids fishing to a jetty in Fremantle. They were not having much luck that day until Alisha finally hooked a monster 'Norwest Blowie' on her line. She was struggling to reel it in by herself, so she passed her rod to Lucas to try, but he could not manage it either.

The fish was thrashing about, when a passing tourist had seen their attempts and offered his help (otherwise Lucas would have to cut the line to retrieve the rod). So, the tourist held onto Lucas' feet, enabling him to dangle over the side of the jetty, pull the line in by hand, till he could grab onto fish with the 'fish grips' and finally land it on the jetty. It was a massive fish! The tourist joined in their excitement and wanted me to take a photo on his camera with the fish, the kids and himself. They continued to argue about who actually caught the fish that day, Alisha who hooked it, or Lucas that brought it in?

Senior school had finally started for Lucas with excitement and slight trepidation. As was part of the Corpus tradition, some Year 10 students who volunteered as Quest Leaders, helped manage the incoming Year 7 students on their Quest Retreat - a neighbourhood can collection for charity. Lucas enjoyed being a Quest Leader and had a great time mentoring his group of Year 7's.

Shortly after Valentine's day Lucas started seeing a girl in his year group from school. Although this didn't last very long, they remained good friends.

He surprised himself, realising he was actually pretty good at tennis and became part of the Senior School Tennis Team. As a few of The Boys played for clubs, they would meet every now and then for a fun game at the local tennis club that some of them belonged to.

Alisha had been diagnosed with Type 1 Diabetes since she was 4, so Lucas had seen her grow up with this terrible chronic affliction and always encouraged her to be vigilant about testing herself. He would randomly ask her to take *his* finger prick to see what his blood sugar levels were. He even voluntarily injected himself, as did Les &

myself, when she was younger to reassure her and show her how easy it was to do. Lucas had watched us inject Alisha's insulin for years and also learnt what to do. Alisha had finally agreed to let him inject her insulin with us guiding him. This was a huge step for all of us and it gave Lucas a sense of empowerment and a way of helping his sister, until she was ready to begin injecting herself.

Not wanting to do much for his 15th birthday, we celebrated at home with my parents over afternoon tea. Alisha had proudly made Lucas' birthday cake for him, which he was wrapped with.

Around this time was when he changed from wanting to be an Architect to an Engineer. He was enjoying school and had a good understanding of all his subjects so he definitely had the capability to become an Engineer if he kept heading in the same direction.

During the year Lucas and his friend Peter had joined the EV (Electric Vehicle) challenge at school. This involved them mentoring and helping younger students to build and race an electric vehicle. They did this after school one or two days a week. When the vehicle was assembled enough to ride, one of the younger students was desperate to drive it in the school grounds. Whilst driving he lost control of it, which sent Lucas and Peter running madly after him as he was headed straight for glass doors. He narrowly escaped the doors as he managed to swerve the vehicle the other way in time. It would have been the end of the vehicle, the glass doors and them, as they were 'in charge'!

Lucas had been talking about getting a part time job now that he was 15. Les had discussed this with him and suggested that he work on Saturdays at *his* workshop with him. He began his first job for his dad at then called Project Painting Services. He did all the mundane jobs like moving boxes, pumping vehicle tyres and other general odd jobs. Lucas' friend Ricky also came to work with Les and Lucas. Along with lots of laughs and a *bit* of hard work, these two boys looked forward to lunch time when Les would bring Red Rooster back for them!

As part of their school commitment, Lucas' year group was required to work a certain number of hours 'community service' and the kids were given a choice of the work they wanted to provide. Lucas chose his service at the Epiphany Retreat Centre which basically needed a massive yard clean-up. At the end of the day when I came to pick him up, to my surprise, I saw him with a big smile on his face driving the yard tractor with the trailer attached, piled high with branches. Then another lap, this time some of the girls hitching a ride in the trailer, he was in his element!

Year 10 seemed to be the year of partying and socialising. Luckily for him he was working hard at school and doing well too. By third term he had again received the Indonesian award.

At work, after repainting the workshop wall and floors and various other jobs that needed attending, Les was running out of odd jobs for the boys to do. Lucas and Ricky had both been given a taste now of what working was like. After Les advised them things would be winding down for them, Ricky eventually found another job at Hoyts and Lucas at Southside Pool Services in Canning Vale.

Peter Schmidt, the owner of Southside Pools wanted a reliable part timer who had good Chemistry and Maths knowledge - an easy fit for Lucas. He started with basic jobs like stocking shelves and carrying bags of salt to customer's cars. And eventually learnt how to perform water tests and was serving people and providing advice at the counter. He had a great work ethic and was highly regarded by his co-workers *and* the ladies in the café he frequented next door! He was so proud of his job and enjoyed being part of the team too.

In September we took a holiday to Kuala Lumpur. We visited

Sunway Lagoon which boasted a massive outdoor wave pool. With the sound of an alarm, swimmers wait in anticipation for the next round of waves to begin. It was exciting to brace for them, waiting for wave upon wave to crash and hurling those that weren't ready for it through the water. Poor Alisha being the smallest of us was dumped by the waves the most, but all of us loving the awesome fun of this place.

Lucas really wanted to try bungee jumping too at Sunway Lagoon. After Les and I agreed, (me regrettably), he climbed a seriously tall tower, and after being prepped on what to do, jumped. It was both nerve wracking but thrilling to watch and he was exhilarated afterwards!

The end of the year school awards ceremony saw him nominated again for the Mary of the Cross all round award. He also received the Indonesian award and plaque for the year. And then enjoyed the long awaited Year 10 river cruise, even with its daggy music.

We rounded the year off by going to Cebu in the Philippines for Christmas and stopping over in Singapore. Cebu is a world class diving destination, where Lucas and Les took underwater photos and videos of their dive. They were totally ecstatic afterwards and Les was so glad that Lucas convinced him to go.

But Cebu is also a scary place to be, kidnapping is common, poverty prevalent and people gun crazy. The only place we actually felt safe was within our hotel. The hotel security was extreme, with the guards checking the underneath of all vehicles entering the Shangri La for explosives, something we had never experienced before. Whenever we travelled by taxi through the city, people on the streets approached the taxi begging for money, an eye-opener for the kids. At shopping centres security guards scanned everyone for guns or explosives before allowing them to enter the centre, but when you were inside, Lucas found a shop where you could buy all sorts of guns and ammunition in all sorts of sizes - insane!

Les had to look at and quote a job in Cape Leveque (north WA). He decided to take Lucas along with him for the experience of it. It was memorable for Lucas, in the way of being eaten by mosquitoes within the confines of their eco-style accommodation.

Just prior to Year 11 commencing we received a letter from Corpus inviting Lucas to join the school's exclusive Excelsis Club, that brought together a group of high achieving students. We were thrilled and I had always felt he would become part of this club, which rewarded his hard work and dedication to his studies. These club members met weekly after school, for group discussions and specialist advice in any subject they required and sometimes had guest speakers attend also. But really, Lucas was there for the food!

Alisha had started Year 7 at Corpus now too and loved it when Lucas would stop to acknowledge her, or have a chat when they saw each other at school. Alisha loved having her big brother around at school and his friends got to know her too. She knew so many of the Year 12's through Lucas, many of the girls coming up and hugging her which made her feel special. She would quite often buy Lucas something from the canteen after school before she came to the car at pick up time.

Around this time he starting seeing a girl in his year group, but after a brief time it ended, them remaining friends afterwards though.

When he turned 16, all he wanted to do for his birthday was get his 'L's' (Learner's permit). He booked in and we went to the licensing centre straight after school that day to apply for it. When we got home I took him out for his first 'legal drive' around the block a few times (his GTA Xbox training had obviously paid off!) Les was working away at the time and when he returned a few days later, he took him out for his first 'official' driving lesson. Lucas proudly picked up his first car (a black Holden Cruze) not long after that with Les. And Alisha again made his birthday cake, this time a GTA cake, that blew him away.

Lucas and a couple of his friends helped some of the Science teachers develop the school's Astronomy group. They would meet at night with some of the teachers to set up a new high-powered telescope that the school had just purchased. Once they had worked it out they assisted the Astronomy students from younger years to use it.

He was on top of the world now, working, driving, socialising, doing well at school and finally had his braces removed too!

The Year 11 Dinner Dance was the social event of the year. The kids all enjoyed getting dressed up for this. The girls always did, but the boys had finally caught up with them and got on board with this 'dressing up' stuff too.

Year 11 was crammed into three terms instead of four, allowing Year 12 studies to commence in term four, permitting more time for Year 12 studies. So in fourth term Lucas and his fellow homeroom friend Nicole were chosen as Year 12 Prefects to represent their house Merici, with Ricky also being chosen for his house MacKillop. Many of the prefects chosen for the other houses were Lucas' friends also. They were presented with their Prefect badges at the whole school assembly watched on by a very proud Alisha.

In October Les, Lucas and I were out to dinner (Alisha was at a party), when we decided that we would take Lucas into the casino with us. He was 6'3" by now and so looked the part of an adult. I remember Les telling him not to make eye contact with the security at the entry and just walk in confidently. Job accomplished - we were in!

His eyes were popping out of his head with everything going on. We went to the money wheel first which was simple enough for him to work out. He ended up winning 23 to 1 and told us to go on and he would catch up with us, "Not a chance Buddy" was Les' response. Then we showed him the game we like to play Baccarat. He asked me, "If I had a drink in my hand would it look more the part?" to which I'm sure he knew my answer! And of course he proudly bragged to The Boys about his night afterwards.

For Christmas we were back in Exmouth with Les' cousin Melvyn and his wife Delilah joining us. Lucas loved staying at that holiday house on the canals. The sloping backyard with its swimming pool and beyond was the jetty where the boat was ready to go at a moment's notice. When he was not out on the boat, Lucas again spent his time fishing from the jetty.

ENJOYING TIME HOLIDAYING IN EXMOUTH, WA

On Christmas Eve we all went to the only catholic church in Exmouth for mass. Unluckily we had the wrong mass time and when we entered the church (nearly half way through mass), the small but nosey congregation collectively turned around to stare at us. They were friendly enough though, with most of them greeting us with Christmas wishes afterwards.

2016 - YEAR 12 (THE BETTER HALF)

Once again we began 2016 in Denham, Shark Bay just the four of us this time. We were happy to just have this time away together, enjoying boating, fishing, eating and swimming especially at Monkey Mia.

A GREAT CATCH BY LUCAS

An enjoyable school holidays, with the last weekend of holidays being the Year 12 School Ball, held at the Rendezvous Hotel in Scarborough. The excitement of this had been building for months, or *maybe* just for the girls. Lucas was accompanying his friend Nicole to the ball. He looked so handsome in his suit and was slightly nervous when we arrived at Nicole's house, even though he had met her parents several times before over the years. Nicole was stunning in her dress and they both looked so grown up.

After a drink and many photos at Nicole's, both families headed to the "pre's", which was a gathering of all the kids in the group who were going to the ball together in the limousines they had organised (with their excited family members in tow) 'The Boys' were not at these same pre's, as Lucas' were organised by the girls they were partnering - different friends' circles, which is a shame.

Nevertheless, it was pretty exciting seeing all these boys looking so dapper in their suits and the girls so sophisticated in their ball dresses. Les was one of the official photographers for the group, along with Ros and Anthony, Brendon's parents. Once the photos were finished at the pre's, the kids, again followed keenly by their families, went to Monument Hill overlooking Fremantle for more group photos and then *finally* onto the ball itself. This was a special night for our son and I was happy that he was proud to share part of it with his family.

READY FOR THE SCHOOL BALL

After the ball, the kids all headed to their chosen "afters" parties at various people's houses. As a lot of the kids had already turned 18 there would be alcohol at the parties, which Lucas had mentioned to us beforehand, but as he had always been very sensible, we were not overly concerned and he ended up having a great night.

With the school ball finally out of the way, the year group finally began their last year of high school together. Lucas really 'came into his own this year'. He was a Year 12 Prefect, a special minister of holy communion, doing extremely well academically, whilst managing his work commitments and was really enjoying his final year. As a Prefect he spoke at assemblies, addressing his house, year group or whole school. He had the respect of students and teachers alike.

Only a few weeks into the new school year was the interhouse swimming carnival. Lucas' house Merici were the winners of the carnival, with Lucas and Nicole, the Merici Prefects, being awarded the swimming shield, with Alisha proudly looking on.

Then followed the senior school cross country. Not being particularly 'into' athletics Lucas didn't really take things too seriously, but was happy enough to participate. Being his last cross country carnival I went to spectate. Lucas had told me he and The Boys planned to yell out "Allahu Akbar" when the starter's pistol went off at the beginning of the race, as a joke. Which they did, pretty loudly, laughing at the same time and blending into the whole sea of Year 12 boys before teachers could single anyone out!

The Boys created a dud ceremony in Year 11 & 12 called the Doumbia awards. This involved them and many of the boys from their year group gathering at lunch time, donning bow ties and holding a ceremony to hand out random goofy/bad awards. There were many other crazy antics they got up to when they were all together and hearing their witty 'banter' made me smile. Lucas loved these boys and they meant the world to him and vice versa.

YEAR 12 – (2ND HALF OF THE YEAR)

It was a week before the July school holidays commenced that Lucas' cancer diagnosis was made. A devastating time in anyone's life, but one made so much worse as he was in his last year of high school with final exams looming. The Boys came around to our house the following night as they wanted to be with their mate. Leaving them to the privacy of our theatre room, there was still plenty of laughter going on under such crappy circumstances and they Xboxed through the evening too, which helped Lucas so much.

We advised school of what he was about to undergo, as he would probably need a fair time away from school. Les also advised Peter from Southside Pool Services that Lucas would no longer be able to work there. Peter suggested he take as much time as he needed and told us that he would hold his job open for him for a year - unbelievable compassion from Lucas' employer, that he was so grateful for!

His high dose chemotherapy treatment required him to be an 'inpatient' in hospital for usually a week at a time and then was terribly sick for a week or two after each chemo round, so missed a lot of term 3 & 4 at school.

During his treatment he was still dedicated and driven to study towards his final ATAR exams, as he had the sheer determination of attaining his much dreamed of Engineering degree at Curtin University.

Together with plenty of emails to and from his subject teachers at school, he was also helped along by the wonderful teaching staff from the hospital, mainly at his bedside, so he was able to keep up with schoolwork. To his credit Lucas pushed through his treatment and operation as best he could and when he was able to, attended school to the surprise and delight of The Boys and many other friends.

One time after being discharged from hospital, it was his final school athletics carnival and he really wanted to go there, before going home, so we did. His friends were all so happy to see him, albeit in his normal clothes and beanie instead of school sport uniform. He even had the chance to join in the Year 12 Prefect egg and spoon race which was perfect!

The Year 12 Graduation was a special but somewhat disappointing time for Lucas. He was proud to be graduating and for everything he had achieved in high school, but was annoyed and frustrated at having to attend the Graduation Mass at St Mary's Cathedral bald, in a wheelchair and then having to use crutches for this significant occasion.

Before their final day at school, the prefects were required to stay back after school and help set up for the graduation day breakfast for the following morning. As he could not physically help, he still remained after school and helped the others out in whatever ways he could.

Les, Alisha and I were so proud of him at the final graduation assembly. He was wheeled into the school gym by his friend Peter who was also part of his Merici homeroom group. Lucas was nominated for the Sequere Dominum Award (the highest award at school), for which he received a medal and certificate. It took a lot of courage for him to stand before his whole school cohort and parents, with a bald head and crutches. Especially as he had missed so much school since July and a lot of the students were unaware of his medical situation. Still, he proudly got up there and did it!

The end of the ceremony culminated in the graduating class leaving the school gym in a procession headed by Lucas in his wheelchair being pushed by Peter, such a gorgeous moment! There was lots of excitement and cheering from a guard of honour made by the parents. The kids all then released balloons in their house colours into the sky. We took many proud photo's to remember this special day, but I always felt like Lucas looked slightly disappointed in these shots. Alisha was excited and extremely proud of her brother who she had always looked up to and this day was special for her too.

When the festivities of the day finished, a lot of the kids were heading to the beach to celebrate, as was tradition. This sadly was not an option for Lucas because of the wheelchair. I tried to make him feel a little better by taking him to lunch at Bluewater Grill, which has a beautiful view of the river and city and it was a such a lovely day too. He was very grateful for this, but it saddens me still that he missed out on the fun with his friends, who understandably, he would much rather be with.

With graduation over, the final ATAR exams were upon him. (A month or so earlier the mock/trial exams took place, but as Lucas had just had surgery on his leg that week, he was exempt from sitting these). The final ATAR exams meant everything to him. But because he was scheduled to be in hospital on treatment during this time, we organised a mountain of paperwork to be signed off by doctors, the hospital and school, that gave him 'special consideration' with SCSA (School Curriculum and Standards Authority) prior to the exams in such extraordinary circumstances.

It also meant that he would need to sit the exams 'on site' in hospital. As if the normal stress of these exams was not enough! (He had attended the oral Indonesian exam at Tuart College a couple of weeks earlier and hated the fact that students from other schools were staring at him because he was bald and using a wheelchair).

It was a relentless feeling for him whenever he was around particularly people of his own age group, who didn't know what was going on with him. He didn't want anyone's pity, he just wanted to be over this whole ordeal and be able to look and feel normal again!

He continued to study right up to his ATAR exam time, but unfortunately was able to sit only one out of the six ATAR exams (being Religion ironically!), as he was so sick from chemo for the rest of the scheduled dates. Still following all the normal protocol of the exams, he sat the Religion exam in a room in the offices of the hospital's teaching staff, along with another girl Kate, who was also going through chemo. Even this was a battle as he was in a wheelchair and not able to be comfortable for a three hour exam. He was so disappointed at not being able to complete the rest of his exams that he had worked so hard towards.

To his credit and his amazing schoolwork ethic and drive, after the 'special consideration' was applied, he achieved the amazing ATAR score of 91.8, a high ATAR by any standard, let alone someone going through chemo and the challenges of the previous 5 months! We were so proud of him and all he had achieved through hard work, dedication and perseverance. His name was listed amongst the high achieving students from Corpus in the newspaper.

Then he received confirmation that he had been accepted into his university of choice, Curtin, to study a Bachelor of Engineering (Honours) degree which he had been striving towards. What an achievement, but it was bittersweet, as he had to then make the agonising decision to defer for a year, as he was only scheduled to finish chemo the beginning of the following year (2017) and would need the time for rehabilitation and rebuilding his strength. If he didn't have to defer he would have been in the same university course as his mate Peter.

The other thing Lucas had to miss was going to 'Leavers' - the end of school celebrations that many graduates looked forward to. Lucas was the one from The Boys who had organized the house for them all to stay in for the festivities in Busselton (south of Perth). There was no way that it would be safe in the drunken teenage crowds for someone who had been through chemo and 'limb salvage surgery', to be there in a wheelchair or crutches. As it turned out he had chemo scheduled for that week so there was no chance of him going anyway, just another blow to a non-existent end of year celebration and all the associated parties he also had to forego.

He finally got his 'P plates', which meant he would be able to drive on his own now. Only to be disappointed again, as he was not yet able to drive due to his leg surgery and the accumulated effects of chemo.

As Lucas was in hospital the week before Christmas we saw the very touching and amazing generosity of people to the patients in the oncology ward. Lucas would receive a gift almost every day during that week leading up to Christmas. We were also lucky enough to have a *private* orchestra visit and a mini concert in Lucas' hospital room by members of the WA Symphony Orchestra. Alisha thought she would bring some Christmas cheer to his room by decorating it with handmade paper decorations, that we hung from every possible spot.

Thankfully Lucas was discharged from hospital in time to spend Christmas with us. As we couldn't go away for Christmas this year as we would normally do, we spent Christmas in the newly opened Crown Towers and New Years in the Crown Metropol, enjoying being together as a family again at the end of a crazy year.

So, the year that began with so much promise had been such a difficult one for him. He still however managed to enjoy a lot of fun times with friends and family and a fantastic result academically, despite all the hardship he endured.

CHAPTER SEVEN

New Hope

The new year began with new hope and optimism that this year would be a much better one than the last.

Lucas was happy to catch up with The Boys when he was able to and he always looked forward to the limited times he could. He was doing well, despite the many side effects and just wanted this all to be over so he could get on with things. He had a great outlook on life and as much as he hated cancer and what it had put him through, he was not going to let it stand in his way.

Although he was not hospitalized during January, he still had to attend ongoing testing regarding his treatment and was relieved that these tests allowed him to return home the same day.

Renal tests indicated that Lucas' kidneys were not coping as well as they had hoped. We saw the renal doctor in mid January who advised that the kidney's function of flushing the toxins out of his body was compromised. There was a possibility that his kidneys could possibly resolve this problem in time, on their own accord, but if not, he was looking at the prospect of kidney dialysis - obviously a big worry to us all.

February 2017

Further tests were conducted in February, as was usual prior to the next round of in-patient chemo treatment. His mood and mindset were positive and strong before this round. He just wanted to get through these last few rounds so he could be done with treatment.

After this round finished, his kidneys were still unable to flush the toxins from his body, so he had to remain in hospital. It was decided that he would now need intermittent dialysis which had to be done every few days in ICU (Intensive Care Unit), as the dialysis machine in ICU was gentler on his heart than the ones in the renal ward.

But before this could be done, he required surgery for a new port for dialysis access (this was the opposite side from the port already there for chemo access). But due to his weakened heart he was only given a local anaesthetic rather than a general, when the port surgery was done, to which he had many adverse reactions! After his surgery he began a new regime of movement between the oncology ward and ICU for weeks on end, during which he was bedridden.

Family, friends and The Boys had been to visit a number of times, but as Lucas was not in a good way he didn't want people seeing him like this and didn't want any other visitors for the most part also. The Boys kept his spirits up through their online banter with him when he was up to it.

March 2017

The decision was then made that instead of transferring him to and from ICU that he would remain in an 'isolated' room in ICU as he was now also immune compromised. This tiny room was filled to capacity with his specially equipped bed (for which he needed an extension because of his size), the dialysis machine and all the other specialist ICU equipment in the room. When family or friends did come to visit him in ICU, I had forgotten how confronting it must have been for them, as I had just become so used to the equipment and what went on in there.

I had also come to know the ICU staff as he was there so often and now a 'fixture' to the area. They are an amazing group of dedicated people who were so caring, showing such a compassionate side of nursing at such a vulnerable time for the Child patients they cared for, along with their parents.

During this stressful time, our new house that we had been waiting 2 years to be built was finally completed. We moved in on 3/3/17, right when Lucas was critical in ICU. Because things had been so dramatic in the previous few weeks, I was struggling to finish packing, let alone move. But we did it – we finally moved to our new home that was designed by Lucas and Les together. Alisha had excitingly set up Lucas' new bedroom for him. She was meticulous in hanging or folding clothes and storing his shoes. His walk-in cupboard shelves proudly displayed all his medals, trophies, photo's and everything precious to Lucas on them. She was so proud of her efforts that she videoed his room and sent it to me so I could show him. But he said he didn't want to see it then, instead saying "No leave it, I want it to be a surprise".

From mid March Lucas was on daily intensive dialysis. He had also contracted some type of lung infection which required a CT guided lung biopsy, again only under local anaesthetic. Family took turns in coming into ICU and sitting with Lucas and myself/Les (only two visitors were allowed at a time in ICU).

As the situation had turned dire, a meeting was then arranged with all the different teams that were now involved in Lucas' care - the ICU team, the Oncology team, Pain Management team, Renal team, Cardiac team, and Dietician team. His condition was deteriorating and so was his energy. A week later he was gone.

PART TWO

*(Part Two involves a detailed account of what
happened to Lucas from diagnosis onward)*

CHAPTER EIGHT

Diagnosis

L ucas complained of a sore knee in late June 2016. I remember telling him to "Put some balm on it," as kids are always getting knocks or pains here and there. The pain subsided for about a week, then returned when he was at school. He messaged me during the day saying the pain was really bad and could I make a doctor's appointment for him. This child had rarely been to the doctor's in his life, just the odd sickness here and there over the years, so I knew if he had asked he really needed a doctor!

Our usual doctor was not available, so I booked in to see Dr Mandic, who I have previously seen. After a few questions from her she referred Lucas for an X-ray and CT scans, nothing unusual about this request.

Lucas had the scans the following day. Alisha waited in the car while I took Lucas in. He went in for the scans on his own and we just needed to wait for the report at the conclusion of his appointment. However, the Radiologist came out saying "Lucas you stay there, mum can you come in please?" I knew this could not be good, as I faked giving Lucas a reassuring look.

When I entered her room she had his scans on her screen. She told me that she had just been in touch with Lucas' doctor and that she would like us to go straight to the hospital for an MRI, as they had found a lesion on his bone. I was totally confused and asked her if it looked sinister and she showed me a mass protruding from his knee bone and said that it was not good. I recall feeling overwhelmed with shock and confusion as I walked out of her room, Lucas looking at me with a worried face made it so much worse.

Not really comprehending what was just said, I explained to him exactly what she had told me and saw the fear and panic on his face. Alisha was just annoyed at how long it all took, though she could see we were worried and was asking what was going on.

I decided to call Dr Mandic first, before we began driving to the hospital. I was put through to her directly, which in itself is unusual in a doctor's surgery. She told me that it was probably too late in the day for an MRI to be arranged at the hospital and we should just come in to the surgery for a chat.

By the time the three of us arrived at the surgery all the other patients had left. The administration staff, who I had known for years, were looking at us sympathetically, which was also not a good sign and we were ushered into Dr Mandic's room straight away.

Lucas, Alisha and I sat silently in her room, while she basically told us the news. Pointing to his scans on her screen and after speaking with the Radiologist, they had concluded, through their combined experience that it looked like a bone tumour. I went numb, as I just could not register what that actually meant. She explained that in her opinion, she thought it might be either Ewing sarcoma, osteosarcoma (both bone cancers) or osteomyelitus (a bone infection). Lucas was frozen in his seat – he was in total shock! I put my arm around him and said "It'll be ok, let's get the tests done first." Stupid thing to say and really does not mean much when you've been told you could have cancer. Every other possibility seems to drop away and they are the words that stay with you. I held his hand for the remainder of the time in that room, while Dr Mandic explained that the tests would happen quickly as these were aggressive sicknesses! Alisha looked as scared and worried as Lucas and myself by now at the seriousness of it all.

I will always remember the way Dr Mandic handled telling us such devastating news, professionally, but with such compassion. She was so apologetic for having to deliver this information to us. You could see her genuine concern for Lucas, Alisha and myself.

When the three of us returned to the car to drive home, I saw that Lucas had tears in his eyes. I hugged him and said he was going to be ok. What a thing a 17year old had been thrown to deal with! Alisha was pretty quiet in the car as we all tried to manage the gravity of it.

Les was working away at the time and had known we were going to have the X-ray that day and just happened to ring at that moment. He asked how it all went and I told him that we had just been at the doctor's and that they think he might have cancer in his leg. He said "Yeah right, don't joke about things like that". As I explained it to him, I felt my heart breaking and could not stop the tears from rolling down, even though I had so desperately not wanted to cry in front of Lucas. We sat in the car, all of us devastated and teary and Les the same on the other end of the line.

By the time we got home everyone was over emotional and tired. It had been such confronting news and obviously not what we had been expecting from some pain in the knee! Lucas went to his room for a while and I cried uncontrollably in my bathroom (so the kids did not know). I called Les back and talked about it some more and we agonised over it together.

When Lucas came out of his room he said to me "Do you know what the Spanish word for cancer is? It's El cancer!" and laughed his hearty laugh. This boy was amazing, obviously further testing was yet to be performed, but the sheer genius of him using humour as a coping strategy was awesome. Later in the evening when I asked him as usual, to take the bin out, he came back with "I can't, I have cancer!" – classic Lucas!

The following day I was informed of the numerous test arrangements. Les in the meantime, was not coping well with being away 'on site' whilst all this was happening. As it was nearly the end of the contract he was working on, his awesome employees told him to go home and be with us and they would take care of things at work for him.

Lucas had further X-rays, CT scans, a biopsy, a PET scan and fertility samples taken also. Unbelievable and invasive what he was now having to go through. We made a decision as a family not to say anything to anyone else until we had all the results. Lucas could do without the input from everybody else while he was waiting anxiously for the results. This painful and distressing week seemed to take forever to pass.

Finally on 6/7/16 we had the diagnosis we did not want. It was osteosarcoma of the left knee. A malignant tumour was growing from inside and protruding out of his femur bone. The Orthopaedic Surgeon who would be performing Lucas' 'limb salvage surgery' as it is known, gave us the diagnosis. This would involve the removal of the tumour and the replacement of the femur and tibia bones with metal prosthetics – major surgery. Before he could have surgery, he would need three months of high dose chemotherapy and another three months after.

I remember the surgeon telling me to breathe now, as he could see the obvious pain on my face. He was confident that he was going to "Fix Lucas and all would be ok." Lucas turned and hugged me, *I* should have been hugging *him*! Les was stunned and fairly quiet, trying to process it all and be strong for Lucas and myself.

After the surgeon explained the complex the surgery, recovery and rehabilitation with us, a very caring Specialist Cancer Nurse, took over and guided us through further conversation at the Youth Cancer Unit of the hospital. She understood our shock and uncertainty and spoke to us as a family of how we could support Lucas and each other during this time.

Whilst we were talking with her I noticed Lucas acknowledge (with a nod of his head), a fellow Year 11 student from Corpus, James. Lucas had previously mentioned to me about James going through treatment. Meanwhile the nurse spoke to Alisha asking what school she goes to. When Alisha answered, a lady standing nearby overheard and came over to us saying her son James goes to Corpus and introduced herself to us as Kerry. Lucas told her that he had just seen James. Kerry told us a little about James' ordeal and kindly gave me her phone number and to call her if I needed to chat, as it was a tough road ahead. A few weeks into Lucas' treatment I called Kerry and we became friends.

We were given the choice of two hospitals for his treatment, but we left that choice to Lucas. He of course chose the one who had access to teachers and supported school work, as he was in the middle of his final year of high school and was adamant that 'this' would not interfere with his academic ability. We then were guided to the appropriate hospital where we had a brief and overwhelming meeting with his primary Oncologist.

After an exhausting day we then had to tell this devastating news to our families, who were understandably upset. Lucas chose to share his diagnosis with The Boys and only a few other close friends. He was not one for all the sympathy and just wanted this to all be over. He was determined to do well in his ATAR and get his place at Curtin University studying Engineering. This was a huge curveball that he was going to struggle through but overcome!

CHAPTER NINE

Treatment

A few days before chemotherapy treatment could begin, I took Lucas to the hospital to have a type of drip inserted on his arm, which would be used to give various medications and take bloods during his treatment. Even though this was done in the 'same day' treatment room (in the oncology ward), it was confronting for us seeing kids coming and going from the room for various treatments or procedures, many visibly ill and with either partial or no hair. Nothing can prepare you for this, especially the fact that it's happening to either babies, young children or teens, as was the case in this hospital. After taking in so much, we were glad when we could go home when it was over for the day. That evening Peter, Ricky and Joseph came to visit Lucas at home. They played Xbox, stuffed themselves on pizza and laughed and joked as normal, just what Lucas needed.

Knowing that it was inevitable that he would lose his hair at some stage during chemo, Lucas made the tough decision to shave his hair short. Les did this for him which was distressing for all of us, as the reality of it all had begun to set in. Lucas loved his hair and had just told us in his humorous way "Aww, just when I was trying to grow my fringe longer!"

The following week 12/7/16 he was admitted to hospital early morning, as he required surgery before chemo could begin. Les took him this time and the surgery was to insert a 'port' into his upper chest. The port was inserted under his skin and the tubing from it into his neck. Basically, this meant that nurses could then just 'needle' through his chest into the port (kind of like 'plugging in') whenever chemo was required.

With surgery complete, later in the day he was admitted to the adolescent side of the ward (the other side being for babies and younger children) whilst he was still recovering. Most rooms in the adolescent ward had two beds to a room and there were also two 'isolation rooms' for patients that had compromised immune systems, but luckily that first day he did not have anyone sharing the room with him.

By the time Alisha and I came to the hospital after her day at school, Lucas was still extremely groggy, angry and was definitely not himself. Everything we did annoyed him. We were trying to have some fun with him, as usual, but he was in no mood for it. The chest surgery site was painful and his arm drip was attached to a portable pump stand sending fluids through his body, so that really annoyed him too. When the hospital food came around he was not interested in eating and was not able to feed himself anyway, so Alisha offered to feed him. Which was alright at first, until he started to become angry with her for every little thing.

Some of the Dockers (football team) came into the oncology ward to visit the kids in treatment. Lucas was too blurry to care and as we're not big football fans we weren't fussed. They came into his room to speak to us, but I told them not to worry as he was too unwell, there were plenty of other kids for them to spend time with.

Later that night his chemo was to begin, incredibly unfair as he was in so much pain still. But the doctors had advised us that no time could be wasted as his cancer was aggressive. They were also worried about it metastasizing (spreading) to other sites in his body. I stayed on the couch next to him that night, watching attentively all that was happening to him.

Before chemo could begin he needed to be hydrated, so that meant the flow rate of saline fluids were increased to a staggering 410ml/hr and the loud sound of his vigorously operating pump, became the dominant sound in his otherwise silent room. This in turn meant he needed to use the toilet every half hour or so which was a real feat for him. As chemo may also causes nausea, he was given anti-nausea drugs to help counteract it, adding to his fogginess now too. The only positive of this was the bathroom was his alone for that first night at least!

His actual chemo did not start till much later at night. I watched as two nurses were required to administer the chemo drugs, checking everything. The nurse that actually attaches the bag of chemo to the pump, was required to wear protective safety glasses, gloves and a gown. It was unnerving to see this protective gear being worn by the person, who at the same time is infusing that toxin into your child's body. The actual chemo drug bag is then covered by another blue plastic bag as it is sensitive to light and has 'cytotoxic' written boldly on it in large letters. It was a very daunting and confronting thing for me to see, let alone Lucas as a 17year old boy!

It is horrible as a parent to know that your child is effectively being poisoned, as that is essentially the nature of chemo drugs. The drugs are designed to kill and destroy cancer cells, but in doing so, also destroy healthy cells in the body too. In this day and age it seems unreasonable, but this is the protocol that was to be followed. We as parents had little choice, either we use this way that is professionally recognized and recommended, or risk any consequences of this merciless disease.

The chemo treatment Lucas needed as an inpatient required the nurses to measure and record all input and output from him. Input being drugs, fluids, food, drinks etc and output being anything that is released from the body. There are 'pan rooms' in the oncology ward, where weary eyed parents pass each other during the night carrying their child's 'output' in disgusting disposable cardboard holders, so the nurses can record the quantity of it.

The nurses suggested to Lucas to make things easier for him, instead of actually using the "wee bottles" (as they referred to them) in the toilet, they could just draw the curtains around him and he could use them whilst he was in bed. There was no way Lucas' pride would allow for this most humiliating of tasks. So, I tried to help my weak, post operative, chemo infused, 17 year old son, to struggle and get out of bed every half an hour and watch him wheel his heavy laden pump stand with wires connected to him, into the privacy of the bathroom and then settle him back into his bed again. That first night went on forever with the constant, loud sound from the pump, nurses frequently in and out of the room checking his statistics, changing medications and resetting the pump and Lucas up every half an hour or so. By morning we were both shattered, him obviously so much more than me.

Les and I tag teamed as I went home to try and get some rest from my zombie-like state and he stayed with Lucas during the day. Alisha and I went back to the hospital with a helium balloon in tow, after school and homework were over. Lucas was still grumpy and extremely tired. I came to find out later that the steroids he had been given contributed to his moods and anger. The worst was this whole chemo procedure would need to be repeated again that night too, which he was most definitely not looking forward to.

When it came to showering time in hospital, the drip connected to his arm and his chest port site needed to be covered with plastic covers, which were ineffectively waterproof. He also had the pump stand just out of the water's reach in the bathroom, as the pump and wires were still attached to him. This was not an easy thing to do whilst feeling dizzy, nauseous and a slurry of many other emotions seething through his body along with the constant fluids and chemo drugs.

Each day whilst he was in his shower, I took on the job of remaking his bed with fresh sheets, the nurses did not need to perform such trivial tasks when they were so busy and at least I could feel useful in some way. As he was so tall, Lucas also did not fit in a normal size bed, so we had to fit an extension to his bed. That way he at least had enough room and could be semi comfortable, given that he could only really sleep on his back, due to the wires attached to his arm and chest.

He also had to use an awful mouthwash every day in order to prevent mouth ulcers (mucositis – a common and painful side effect) from developing. He hated doing this as it left his mouth numb and with a horrible taste.

The balloon Alisha had brought him had to be taken down at his request, as the different drugs he was being given, coupled with the balloon were 'freaking him out.' This goes to show how the otherwise perfectly rational, mind of an intelligent young man can alter when given such powerful drugs.

He was so glad to finally be going home after a week in hospital. Before we left I was given an A4 size ziplock bag from the oncology pharmacy, filled with boxes and bottles of capsules and tablets that he was required to take whilst he was at home! So many, that Les created a spreadsheet so we could keep track of them all, with their ridiculously long names and even longer list of side effects.

When Lucas first came home and was not feeling sick and lying in his bed, Les and I would notice him sitting blankly, gazing into the distance quite frequently. We tried talking to him positively about it, but he did not really engage us. He was angry. His moods were quite erratic from the drugs, so that made things worse. His mind was definitely in a different place now and he was trying to assess and cope with everything that was happening to him. We tried to snap him out of it, but to no avail, so we resorted to laughing at and *with* him about it and this helped to eventually break the cycle. The physical and emotional strain this boy went through was pitiful to watch and we as parents felt totally helpless and this was only the first round!

CHAPTER TEN

Hospital Life

In hospital we met numerous other staff in those first few days which was confusing and overwhelming. Many oncologists, ward doctors, various nursing staff and teaching staff just to name just a few.

Anne Dunnet is the main teacher at the onsite school located in the oncology ward. She sourced the teaching staff Lucas would need to help him with his Year 12 subjects whilst he was an inpatient. Thankfully the bulk of new learning for Year 12 had already been done when he was well and at Corpus and it was mainly revision that was required now. Fortunately, Lucas only needed help with Chemistry and Physics revision and Anne was able to organise these tutors for him, the other subjects he could manage on his own. Most of the time these teachers would tutor him at his bedside as he was too physically sick to sit at a desk and chair.

Each time he came into hospital for another round of treatment, the staff would welcome him back as they soon came to know him well, especially loving his amazing manners and nature. He was like a 'rockstar' as he would walk through the ward to his room, with lots of staff greeting him on the way.

He would always bring with him the school books he would need for the week and went through his notes as much as he could manage when he wasn't feeling too sick or too tired from chemo. Some days he couldn't even manage to look at his iPad because he was feeling so terrible. The teachers often spoke to me about how it was a pleasure to help Lucas, as he actually *wanted* to learn and he was their "Star student!" His motivation to learn was in attaining that Engineering placement at Curtin University.

The adolescent ward was a place where teen patients could come to relax, play games or music, or just have a break from their rooms.

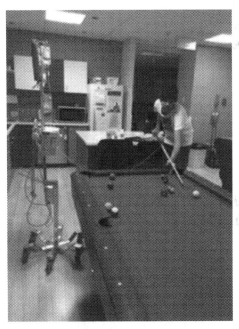

LUCAS PLAYING POOL IN THE ADOLESCENT WARD
WITH HIS CHEMO PUMPS ATTACHED TO HIM

It has its own lounge and kitchen area and it became a regular visiting place for me several times a day. Either to make a quick coffee, store Lucas' food in the fridge, or sometimes to eat my lunch in there, as often Lucas couldn't stand the smell of certain foods in his room. The kitchen area was located right near the teacher's school area and

Anne introduced me to Shani Mulheron who was the English teacher on the ward. Although Lucas didn't need help with English, Shani popped into Lucas' room most days just to have a chat with Lucas, as did Anne.

Anne, Shani and myself chatted each day when Lucas was an inpatient. It was lovely that they both took so much time to talk to us and enquired about Lucas even on days that he wasn't well and not having any tutoring. As strange as hospital life was, it became a second home for me, as so much time was spent there with Lucas. These two ladies helped me more than they will ever know. The amount of times I became teary around them, discussed how ridiculous cancer in kids was and spoke about other 'everyday things' too, was a big comfort to me. Being teachers in a cancer ward, they understood the different cancers and the horrid side effects they can have, because the children they taught often suffered many of them.

I also met many amazing parents in this ward. Maggie and her beautiful, bubbly daughter Catherine. Anthea and Brad, the amazing Paige's parents. Kierstyn and Steve, proud parents of courageous Couper and so many others too. All of us not wanting to be in this place, but unluckily being thrown into it without a choice. The adolescent ward had only a few shared rooms, but the children's wing was even bigger and was so dreadful to see so many cancer kids in it - babies, toddlers and upwards, all going through the same sorts of things as the adolescents, but not understanding it at the same time.

Other lovely people in the ward were the various staff that help clean, deliver food, move beds etc. Two lovely and friendly ladies from this area were Bec and Danuta. Bec, knowing what the hospital's food was like, had learnt to read Lucas' facial expressions when she told him what she had brought him for that particular meal. And Danuta who always had a cheery smile and greeting whenever we saw her. She told me Lucas' lovely nature reminded her of her own son.

Alisha was somehow often around when the food was brought into Lucas' room and after asking him "Are you going to eat that?" happily scoffed away at his unwanted food. As is typical of hospital food, it was quite ordinary and Lucas was frequently either not hungry or 'off' lots of foods from the many nasty chemo side effects. Les and I would often do a 'food run' for him, usually on our way to the hospital. Either picking up an order from a nearby restaurant, or something from a fast food outlet. I continually offered to cook whatever he wanted, but lots of his favourites he now couldn't face, as is the case with many cancer patients. I was always worried about his nutrition when he was in hospital, but was advised that there was not much I could do if he didn't want to eat, so naturally we ended up trying whatever he was *willing* to eat.

Lucas constantly needed bloods taken each time he came into hospital for treatment or even just clinic appointments. This involved going to the hospital's pathology section for either a finger prick test or a syringe to the arm. Although he had done numerous finger pricks at home (encouraging Alisha with her diabetes treatment), he alternated these with syringes initially in hospital.

Also frequently repeated, were CT scans, X-rays, echo's and hearing tests conducted by different areas within the hospital. A baseline round of testing for each one was done prior to chemo beginning and then monitored thereafter. These were usually done with Lucas wheeling his attached pumpstand into the room, then later in a wheelchair *and* pumpstand – a cumbersome feat. He also underwent many radioactive injections of chromium that was visible when scanned and he discussed this with the nuclear medicine staff, as he had some knowledge of this chemical. His height and weight were repeatedly measured when he was on the oncology ward. The nurses always commenting on his immense height, as they struggled to measure him on their tippy toes.

The nurses on the oncology ward were amazing. A dedicated team of staff who were constantly busy and run off their feet. Sarah and Bev were absolutely amazing, friendly and they'd go above and beyond for Lucas. Countless others made this most awful of times, a little more bearable – well for us I'm sure, not Lucas. One of the only male nurses on the ward was Dave, a bearded nurse who looked and sounded more like a 'bikie' than a nurse, but an absolute wealth of knowledge and experience. He would often just chat with Lucas, or when the ward wasn't too busy, sit and watch soccer with him, a comfort for Lucas.

There was a particular friendly oncologist Dr Hetal that we liked too. She was awesome and treated Lucas so well. She had taken the time to get to know Lucas and was aware he was a fishing fanatic and liked watching the fishing shows on TV. She even told him that she started watching 'I Fish' on Lucas' recommendation and said she now understood why *he* liked it.

The Clown Doctors who were mainly there for the little kids, still visited the adolescent ward to try and get the kids to at least smile. They were actually pretty funny – at first! Sometimes when Lucas could hear them approaching his room he would pretend to be asleep or go to the toilet all perfectly timed. They do an amazing job for the kids though.

People who had been touched by cancer in some way, would often donate presents or iTunes vouchers for the adolescents on the ward which is so generous. Especially the teens, as they are often forgotten, as people generally think of 'little kids' when they think of cancer. In some ways it can be worse for the teens, as in Lucas' case, they understand what is happening to them and their bodies and have to mentally cope with it also.

There is a special camp run by the staff from oncology each year, in memory of a boy who passed away from cancer some years ago. A few lucky kids who are not on 'active treatment' at the time are invited to this fully funded adventure. It's a privilege to be asked and is all about having fun and the kids enjoy swimming, fishing and lots of other activities. Lucas was lucky enough to have been chosen to go, but didn't want to, despite the pleading efforts of many staff members.

The other thing that he turned down until I convinced him, was a wish from the Make a Wish Foundation. He didn't think he deserved it and wanted them to grant a wish to one of the younger kids instead. I sent a request to them anyway, wishing for our family to go on a fishing charter up north of WA. He was going through so much and it would be so wonderful for him to have this wish granted. After initially being mad at me for going ahead and requesting the wish, he eventually agreed to it. The Make a Wish people came out and interviewed us and it looked quite hopeful, we would just need to be patient and see what the outcome was.

Lucas surprised me one time when I came to pick him up on a day he was being discharged. His cousin Tash had given him a present of a black afro wig and a red nose for a laugh. I walked into his room and he was sitting there waiting for me in that get up – awesome!

Going in and out of hospital with Lucas for chemo over many months, although a horrific time, showed us what strength, courage, courtesy and pride he maintained at such a difficult time in his life. It was amazing how we became so used to the ups and downs of chemo and hospital life, but we all had the main goal in sight, of getting through this and moving on from here.

CHAPTER ELEVEN

Side Effects

As with a lot of chemo patients, Lucas had begun to feel many shocking side effects. Each chemo drug has it's own set of side effects that each patient may or may not develop. In addition, the many varying medications he was given came with their side effects too. Lucas had all of the side effects I've listed. Although it's distressing I wanted to share what he was enduring, though you wouldn't know it, as he'd just smile and interact as normal in his stoic way when he was feeling well.

A particularly nasty one is mucositis, which is when any part of the body develops multiple painful ulcer like sores. When he had mucositis in his mouth or throat it was covered with these ulcers and made it so difficult for him to swallow, let alone talk or eat. He also had them in his digestive tract at one point.

He needed multiple blood and platelet transfusions during his treatment. He could tolerate these at first, but he eventually developed an allergy to the bloods which showed up as a red rash, so he needed an antihistamine before the transfusion could be given. Then later he developed a reaction to the platelets also.

The one that concerned me from the start was his obvious drop in weight. This was fuelled by a combination of the continual fluids being pumped into him giving him a full, bloated feeling, the nausea and the smell and taste of foods that suppressed his appetite. On the advice of the doctors, as I was constantly questioning them about his eating, or lack of it, they said it was fairly normal and not to be overly worried about it. But to me how could this make any sense? How could his body possibly fight this merciless disease and combat all the drugs he was being given, when he was in such an obviously weakened state, made much worse by little or no nutrition?

The following are a list of the many side effects he had to tolerate

Loss of appetite
Weightloss - 13kg (prior to the 6 weeks he was in ICU)
Loss of Taste
Loss of Smell
Nausea
Vomiting
Dizziness
Constant Tiredness and Fatigue
Weakness
Fevers
Hearing Loss
Tinnitus (Ringing in ears)
Mucositis (Ulcer like sores – mouth & digestive tract)
Hairloss (whole body)
Itchy/Sensitive Scalp
Sore Teeth
Diarrhoea
Belly Pain
Red Coloured Urine (from chemo drugs)
Oily Skin
Sensitive Feet & Fingertips
Replacement of Femur and Tibia Bones with Metal Prosthetics
Inability to Walk

Muscle Loss

Swollen Face, Ankles & Feet

Mood Changes

Some Memory Loss

Loss of Coordination

Reaction to Blood & Platelet Transfusions

Encephalopathy (mild confusion, decreased hand/eye coordination, lethargy)

Inability to urinate

Acute Renal Failure (kidneys)

Chronic Renal Failure (kidneys)

Decreased Heart Function

Bone Marrow Suppression (decreased production of cells for immunity & blood clotting)

Partial Lung Collapse

Unknown Lung Infection

Irregular Heartbeat

Low Blood Sugar Levels

Loss of Voice

Extreme Perspiration

Spitting Blood

Difficulty Breathing

All of this, along with a certain area of the large wound from his leg surgery, that would not heal effectively and his use of crutches and or wheelchair when he was able to move around.

CHAPTER TWELVE

Saving His Leg

Lucas had just undergone three agonising months of chemo and its horrible side effects. As his body was not able to process and flush out the toxins quickly enough, his last round of chemo at this time was cancelled, much to his delight. It was thought that it would not leave ample time to clear through his body before his scheduled surgery date and the surgery was a priority.

The Mock trial exams at school were also scheduled for this same time. After appropriately notifying SCSA, Lucas was exempt from sitting the Mocks. He was not too pleased with this as he wanted to sit through the them as preparation and practice for the final ATAR exams.

After some more routine testing and scans, he was admitted to the hospital where he would have his surgery on 4/10/16. His orthopaedic surgeon was confident that the 'limb salvage surgery' to save his leg would be successful.

After many hours of major surgery, the operation was completed and was a success, with the tumour being removed from his leg. His affected femur and tibia bones were removed and replaced with metal prosthetic parts.

Alisha and I visited him in his hospital room after surgery and we were surprised at how alert he was. He was on very heavy pain killers though, with a fully bandaged leg and was bedridden for the time being, but in good spirits. Les followed on later in the evening and we all stayed with him for most of the night.

The other doctors looking after Lucas in this hospital related well with him. They had even suggested that he tell people that his inevitable scar was from a shark bite, which he liked! They talked with him about what he wanted to do after school. One of them even keen to offer his help to tutor him in Chemistry if he wanted it.

The following day he was able to stand, very slowly, guided by June, the hospital's Physiotherapist. Over the next few days he had to learn how to walk again with the aid of equipment and June encouraging him to try again and again. He wasn't particularly fond of her, (although I think that was because of the medication he was on), so it was a given that Alisha and I began teasing him about her!

He was uncomfortable, in pain, not in a great mind set and really wanted to leave the hospital. Finally, he was discharged and given a huge amount of pain relief to go home with, that he was not keen on taking but we ensured he did. He now had to use a combination of wheelchair and crutches after this, which in itself was so frustrating for him, along with his cumbersome bandaged and extremely sore leg.

Such simple things like having a shower were so dramatic at first, until he was able to build up enough strength to do things himself. We needed to wheel him to our ensuite, as it was more spacious than his bathroom. Then we had to help 'cling wrap' his leg so his bandage wouldn't get wet. Once he was ready, he had to then manoeuvre himself onto a stool in the shower, as he wasn't able to stand. By the time he had finished and got out of his shower, he was exhausted at the effort this was all taking. His mental toughness was also being challenged to the maximum yet again!

Due to the position of his wound (from his upper inner thigh down to the calf of his leg), it was uncomfortable for him to sleep, as he had to try and keep his leg straight. We hired a leg brace support which made things worse for him and he just resolved himself to the fact that he just had to struggle through this part.

A HITH (Hospital in the Home) nurse, Jo, came to check on his wound and change the underneath dressings daily. Eventually we took over this role and later Lucas was able to change the dressings himself.

Next was physiotherapy sessions back at his original hospital. His usual Physiotherapist Jay was on her honeymoon, so Ali was looking after Lucas for the time being. It was a very slow road to recovery, but he was making great progress.

The post op appointment with Lucas' orthopaedic surgeon was positive. He said he had managed to remove the whole tumour, even though it had not shrunk significantly in size, but he was satisfied the margins were clear (meaning the surrounding area). The 'kill rate' of the tumour after chemo was 60%, but they were hoping for closer to 90%. The surgeon was happy the actual operation was a success and the wound was healing well. However, Lucas would still require another three months of chemo as a safety measure. This was to ensure any cancer cells that may have remained behind were killed and therefore not metastasize to any other sites in his body.

By the time Jay returned she was happy to see what Lucas was capable of when he wasn't feeling too sick, as he was already back on chemo again. His did suffer some muscle loss in his leg as expected and Alisha called it his "Girly leg!" Lucas was ok with this, better to make light of it and keep pushing on.

CHAPTER THIRTEEN

Chemo To ICU

Only a week and a half after his major leg surgery Lucas sat his oral ATAR Indonesian exam at Tuart College, where oral exams for all language students were held. He was anxious not only for the exam, but that the many students from other schools also there, were staring at him. *I could even feel all the eyes on him,* as I pushed him in his wheelchair to the designated area. He was glad when it was over as it was a tough exam and was so glad to be leaving this scene behind him.

The following week he was back on chemo and the regime started all over again, now made more difficult by the wound on his leg and his inability to walk unaided.

Fortunately Lucas wasn't hospitalised at the time when the Year 12 Graduation dinner for students and parents, at the Perth Convention Centre was held. He was happy to be *able* to attend, but disappointed by the fact that he was again on crutches and unable to dance and truly enjoy the night as much as he had hoped.

The first two weeks in November were the ATAR exams, which he had been diligently studying for right up to this point. Unfortunately, he was too sick from chemo side effects to be able to sit them and we again had the appropriate clearance from SCSA. He was so disappointed by this, as he truly wanted to show that he was still capable, willing to bear the extreme fatigue and 'chemo fog brain' that he was enduring, but was feeling far too sick to do so. Ironically the only exam he *was* able to sit was the Religion exam. This had to be taken at the teaching staff's offices in the hospital, as he was an inpatient during that time. Same rules applied and a SCSA appointed examiner was sent to oversee the exam, while Lucas and another girl from hospital, Kate, sat their exam's in the same office. He sat uncomfortably through this three hour exam with his pumpstand and wires attached to him, in his wheelchair – not the ideal exam conditions.

Chemo continued on and off over the next few months and he was due to finish his rounds before his 18th birthday at the end of March.

In the car on the way to hospital (13/2/17), he said to me "I don't think I'd go through all this again if the cancer came back". After we discussed it I knew he wasn't upset about it, he was just speaking honestly, saying that as he was nearly an adult the decision would be his after he turned 18, should it ever be required. Later that morning he told me that he had been 'googling' mortality rates for his type of cancer treatment! This was a horrifying moment, to know that my child had been looking at this and was still so brave in the face of it all.

When the oncologist did her daily rounds that same day and saw Lucas and myself on the ward after he was admitted, she informed us that the chemo drugs would be changed this round because of his heart problem. I nearly fell off my chair! I asked her "What heart problem?" and she responded that surely someone would have informed us about it? I told her that we most definitely had not been informed, confirming with Lucas that it was also news to him, for which she apologised! Had we known about a heart problem, we as parents would have been in discussions about it with other professionals and looking into what other options were available

- trying to do something about it! Alarm bells were ringing for both Lucas and myself at that moment, but we were told these new chemo drugs were the best course of action needed now.

I had a private conversation with the oncologist afterward and informed her what he had been telling me in the car about further chemo if the cancer came back and that he had been searching mortality rates. I asked her how far she would push chemo, given all the bad side effects that Lucas had been experiencing. Her reply was "To the point where he doesn't need to question if it came back."

By the end of that round it was clear that the kidneys were not coping. The decision was made in consultation with the hospital's renal team, that as he had acute kidney failure he would need intermittent dialysis to help the kidneys along, in the hope that his kidneys would regain their function. However, given that he apparently had problems with his heart by this stage also, the dialysis would need to be done in the ICU (Intensive Care Unit) of the hospital where the machine would be gentler on his heart. Lucas was shocked by this, but we really had no alternative at this point.

Before dialysis could begin though, he required a temporary 'vascath line' inserted via surgery. This is a venous catheter (plastic tubing) that was inserted in the femoral vein of his groin for access to the dialysis machine. This was performed 'in situ' in his ICU isolation room under local anaesthetic. I was able watch the whole thing whilst holding onto his hand throughout, it was only then that I nearly fainted. With the addition of the vascath, it was yet another thing that had to be covered when he showered making things more uncomfortable for him.

Every couple of days he was transferred (still bedridden), from oncology to ICU for dialysis and then back. The dialysis machine was daunting when I first saw it. This large machine would draw out his blood, filter and clean it and then pump it back into his body. During this process he always felt extremely cold and needed to have a 'bear hugger' machine to warm his body, which was effectively, a thin blow up plastic mattress that pumped warm air through it.

Being transferred back and forth between oncology and ICU meant we came to know the nurses that cared for him in ICU fairly well. They are an amazing and knowledgeable group of dedicated people who genuinely care for their patients. Because Lucas was in there so often they were very good to him and tried to make him as comfortable as was possible in such a crammed isolation room.

One of the most caring nurses that helped him was Chloe, who asked to look after him practically each night. She was into the same sort of movies/TV shows as Lucas. She would often talk to him about Marvel/DC characters and shows and asked him which movie they should watch while she was on her shift. There was also the very knowledgeable Kylie, who made the time to sit and read to him a book she'd brought in for him from her home. Bec, who was so friendly and an immense help to me, (she even baked Lucas cupcakes for his birthday). Gill who was lovely and very helpful and Tracey who talked me through when things became difficult.

Many of our family and Lucas' friends wanted to visit Lucas, but he only wanted them to see him when he was in oncology and not ICU. By this stage though he often didn't feel like seeing anyone and even when he did, wasn't able to engage with them fully as he was feeling so terrible. The Boys, when possible, came to visit him as uneasy and confronting as it was seeing their friend so unwell. Lennon also popped in a few times to encourage him along also (and had previously seen Lucas at home too, when he heard Lucas was sick, on his return from overseas).

As the vascath that was previously inserted was only a temporary measure and Lucas still required more dialysis, a more permanent method was now required. A 'permacath' would need to be inserted via surgery in the nuclear medicine operating rooms of the hospital. This permacath which is a catheter, was placed in the jugular vein of his neck and tunnelled through his chest and out through the chest wall near the collar bone. When we met the surgeon that was to perform this, he said this would normally require general anaesthetic, however in Lucas' case this was not an option due to his decreased heart function, kidney failure and current mucositis in his throat. His surgery would need to be performed under local anaesthetic only, which we were very anxious about.

One of the nurses from ICU was going to be with Lucas for the duration of the surgery. When the surgery was over Lucas was completely traumatized by it. The surgeon was also supposed to remove his vascath, but was unable to do this as it was conveyed to me that Lucas had been through enough. After the surgery I had been told he had become distressed and was hallucinating. Lucas told me that he could feel the whole procedure and was screaming at them to stop, but they kept going. When I questioned this with staff I was told he was hallucinating and was not screaming.

Some time later in ICU, they removed the vascath and Lucas again became very distraught. As I was not present at the time, they also told me that he had been hallucinating and it was possibly from the drugs he was being given.

He'd now developed an unknown lung infection and needed a CT guided lung biopsy, again under local anaesthetic only, due to his heart. When I realised the surgeon was the same as had just done his permacath surgery, I expressed my concern to him that I was not happy with this, due to what happened in the previous surgery. He told me that he was not aware of any of it and said that Lucas had not said anything at all. In the meantime, Sarah and Bev, the two oncology nurses that knew Lucas well, were visibly upset by all Lucas had been through and had rallied the oncology staff, requesting that this not be performed unless it was under a general anaesthetic and a major meeting was held regarding it. They were worried about what it could do to him mentally *and* physically.

A new surgeon explained to me that he had performed CT guided biopsies under local anaesthetic many times, I was a little more at ease then. They would also be using a different local anaesthetic and so should prevent hallucinations.

Before the biopsy could be done, Lucas needed a transfusion of platelets (which he had been given numerous times during his treatment), but this time he had a reaction to it that made him cough profusely. He was given some medication to counteract it and the biopsy was delayed until the reaction had passed. Sarah and I both accompanied Lucas throughout the biopsy, with Sarah holding his hand and encouraging him throughout.

The biopsy showed a partial lung collapse (a type of pneumonia) and the still un-identified chest infection. So again, his medications were increased to try and deal with this also, along with all the other pain medications he was taking. A decision had now been made, as the kidney problems worsened to chronic kidney failure now, that more intensive dialysis was required. This in turn meaning he was permanently in ICU and having daily dialysis.

Lucas was also suffering from terrible mucositis in his throat from the chemo so was not able to eat properly, as swallowing was too difficult, and he also had no appetite. I had always been worried about him not eating and in ICU it was finally recognised as critical and the hospital's dietician's were now involved.

At first, they tried some nutritional supplement drinks which didn't agree with him. As he had lost so much weight already and was very weak by now, they decided he needed a nasogastric tube (soft tubing from his nostril, down the back of his throat, through the oesophagus and into his stomach). This would allow for him to still receive nutrients without him having to eat them.

As the procedure is common and is performed in ICU often, I was prepared to leave to pick Alisha up from school. Although as the nurse tried to insert the tube, it scraped the inside of his nose and due to his platelet count being so low, his blood was unable to clot and caused a nose haemorrhage. They had to 'pack' his nostril with padding to stop further bleeding, this would then be removed in a few days. By the time I returned to the hospital he was again traumatised from all this. He was now on oxygen to help him breathe better, so the sight of the oxygen mask now on his face and his nose 'packed' gave me quite a shock.

He really just wanted to have a shower and feel refreshed after everything. In his weakened state, a nurse and myself helped him into the tiny bathroom that was attached to his very crammed isolation room. Then, temporarily removing his oxygen mask and switching to portable oxygen, removing heart monitor wires, making sure his arm with the drip was covered, along with both chest ports, his leg wrapped in cling wrap and the pumps strategically placed out of the water's reach, he was able to have a somewhat *type of shower*, even though the water was also cold! (the water temperatute was fixed the next day).

Unable to stand by himself, he called me in afterwards to help him get dressed, as he sat on the toilet lid with a towel for some privacy. He was exhausted and out of breath, having to reattach the portable oxygen mask straight away. Such a distressing, sad sight and humiliating for him having to ask for my help, but he said he would rather me than a nurse. I was trying to put on a brave face and get him to think positively that this would at least make him feel a little better.

Even for him to sleep was such a hard thing to do, despite being constantly tired. In ICU the lights are always on, the administering of medications, the constant noises from pumps, heart monitor machines, oxygen machines, the uncomfortableness of his bed (that required tilting to help with his breathing), having to keep his leg straight (because of the wound), lying only on his back (because of the wires attached to him) and with general noise from other patients or nurses, all meant that sleeping was only possible in short spurts. To try and help him sleep, Sarah from oncology came up and gave him her own noise cancelling headphones to use. He was very grateful to her, but was unable to use it, as it was just too uncomfortable on his head which was also very sensitive.

His hands and feet had become very sensitive also. His skin was very dry and cracked and I needed to rub sorbolene cream into his body, especially his legs and feet a few times a day. His wound just would not heal properly in one area, just near the knee joint, so ICU eventually had to call on the Stoma Nurse to review it and have it dressed each day, as she was a specialist in wound care. To add to it he now had an infected ingrown toenail that needed attention. The chest infection and pneumonia were making him continuously cough and he constantly had a build-up of phlegm in his chest which he needed to either spit out or have suctioned out with a machine. Then blood started to appear in the phlegm he was coughing up. He had started to lose coordination of his hands now too. His voice had also started to go, when he *could* breathe and speak we really had to listen hard to understand him. I had to brush his teeth for him, clean his face, cut his nails and wipe his mouth as he was able to do very little for himself now.

A major meeting was held between all the teams looking after him. ICU, the renal team, cardiac team, pain team, dietician and oncology. They would keep going down this track of intensive dialysis for now along with frequent blood and platelet transfusions.

CHAPTER FOURTEEN

Tough Days

Some of the Manchester United soccer players were visiting the hospital and one of the ICU nurses Paul, had organised a visit from them to Lucas. They took a picture with him, gave him a team signed jersey and offered their words of encouragement to him. It was a shame that he wasn't more able to fully appreciate their visit, but he was just too unwell.

As it was apparent things were deteriorating quite rapidly with him, Sarah the amazing oncology nurse, came to visit him in ICU on her day off from work. She was very visibly upset when she spoke with me afterwards, but she was determined to see him. Bev and a number of other oncology nurses wanted to visit him also, but at the time he was not up to seeing anyone else.

Bec, from ICU asked me whilst I was sitting beside Lucas what time Les would be coming in that day. I casually told her it would be on his usual 'evening shift'. She then oddly wanted to know if I knew what time that would be. She gestured towards the door with her head, which Lucas happened to see and he gave me a worried look.

Outside of his tiny isolation room, the ICU consultant doctor and Bec were both waiting for me with a serious look on their faces. They asked me if I would ring Les and ask him to come in sooner as there were a few things that had transpired now, after further test results, which they needed to discuss with us. Obviously, I knew this couldn't be good news as I walked to the corridor to call Les (no mobile phones are permitted in ICU).

Just as I sat down to make the call, Bec happened to walk past and I asked her what was going on. She sat down beside me and held my hand, my heart now racing at the possibilities. I found the courage to ask her the question I really didn't want to know the answer to, "Is he going to die?"

Her reply was a simple "Not today".

I felt my whole body instantly go weak, as if someone had punched me in the stomach and I struggled to comprehend her words. She hugged me in order to try and comfort me, as I looked blankly at her and asked "How can this be happening?"

All she could say was "I know, it's not right, he's your boy." And we sat there in silence, as I wiped away the tears that had flooded my face.

After she left me, ensuring I was 'semi-ok', I realised I still had to make the dreadful phone-call to Les. I just couldn't tell him what Bec had just told me. It would be devastating to hear that over the phone, so I left it out, although he obviously knew that things were of a more serious nature, with a meeting being called and said he would change things around to make it there earlier.

I sat there for a few minutes by myself trying to regain my composure. I knew that I needed my 'game-face' on before I went back into Lucas' room. He had been waiting for me to return and of course asked me what was going on. I lied to him. Saying that they just need to talk to us about some changes. I *know* my son, he wouldn't have believed that and would've been petrified too, but he showed no noticeable sign of it as I walked over and held his hand again.

Les called me back whilst he was driving to the hospital and said that I had him worried. Still, I couldn't give him any more information, as this time, Alisha was in the car with him.

By the time they arrived at the hospital, my mind was a jumbled blur of devastation that Les instantly recognised on my face. After he greeted Lucas with a kiss, Les and I were called away by the doctors whilst Bec stayed with Alisha and Lucas.

In the small interview room which felt void of air, both the ICU consultant and the oncology doctor (Dr Tom, who was rostered on that week) gave us the news that things had taken a turn for the worse and they were "Gravely concerned for Lucas."

The chemo had taken its toll on his body. After five weeks of dialysis and one week of intensive dialysis, his kidneys were chronically failing. This placed extra pressure on his heart and recent tests indicated a very rapid decrease in heart function. This combined with some sort of pneumonia and chest infection, meant the damage to his body was now irreparable. They had never seen this in another cancer patient before, kidneys, heart and lungs all failing. At best they could only try to make him comfortable, but we were really only looking at weeks!

After instantly getting upset, Les asked if we could organise a heart transplant for Lucas, but we were told that wasn't possible as he'd need to be 'cancer free' in order to be eligible. He then said we would take him to another country for a transplant, but we were once again disappointed, being told that the laws were the same internationally.

So as Lucas' parents, we were now helpless to do anything to save our son. The inevitability of this heart-wrenching pain was *one* of the worst feelings I have ever endured, to know that we could not "fix him!"

These revelations stunned me, but I just wouldn't cry. Instead I found myself comforting Les and listening carefully to everything that the doctors were saying, surprising myself. But I was being optimistic too, if they had never seen it in anyone before, there was a chance Lucas could fight this and come through it.

They asked us if we wanted to be there when they told Lucas, as he'd always insisted that the medical staff be straight forward with him. There was no way we were going to let him hear that news alone. When we walked back into his room he knew things were not right. He asked if he was going to die and we just told him to listen to what the doctors had to say. Bec took Alisha outside the room with her at that point.

When he was told all, struggling through his oxygen mask, he just looked down and nodded, almost accepting it. This child was the most amazingly brave person I have and ever *will* know. His reaction was as though they had simply just said something so trivial to him, like you can't watch TV anymore. He should be screaming and crying, or at least be extremely scared, but he was so heroic, he just accepted it as only Lucas could do!

After the doctors left the room, I finally cried and I remember saying to him "Now you need to fight like you've never fought before!", out of sheer desperation and willing positivity. Alisha was devastated when she came back in and heard the news.

The doctors said it would only be weeks, but that didn't make any difference to us. Our precious boy was going to die! There are no words of comfort you can offer a teenager to make any sense of the utter crap of the situation. What he must have been feeling, but decided to internalize still haunts me. I cannot even begin to imagine what he would have been thinking, but he *did* tell Les that he was angry. Angry at the whole course this had taken! That's still hard to forget, that he would die being angry.

Les made the painful calls to notify relatives and very quickly the ICU family waiting room began to fill with our family and friends who had come to see him. Vanessa was one of the first to get to the hospital and remained by our sides. I remember two of The Boys, Peter and James were coming to visit Lucas that evening anyway. When I saw them approaching the corridor I had to give them a quick version of what was going on. They immediately got upset and I hugged them both at the same time. I was comforting boys that should all be out and about having the time of their lives! Instead Lucas' steadfast friends were here, distressed and now had the job of telling their other friends.

Taking it in turns, as only two people could be with him in the room at a time, all our family and friends went in to see Lucas. Distraught and sad, they tried to put on a brave face in front of him. This would have been so difficult for both them and Lucas. What do you actually say to a person in that situation? Anything you say is going to sound insignificant or irrelevant. Mum told me only recently, that during the time she was sitting with him at his bedside, tears running down her face, he said to her "It's ok Nanna." Even during this most tragic of times he still thought of others.

Another patient that was also in ICU had a lot of family gathered outside the ICU main doors. Every time the doors opened, this family were just about falling over each other trying to see inside (a bit like when the doors used to open at the old arrivals hall at the airport). These people were also dark skinned like us and whenever ICU staff came out they would come to our family first and ask if we were the other patient's relatives. To which they were politely told no and pointed towards the other crowd. This provided some light relief at a tense time, until security eventually had to clear them away as they were blocking the corridor and it became a safety hazard.

When Lucas was getting weary from the visitors, Les and I decided to tell everyone to go home as he was tired, as most of them were still in the family room area. But Lucas insisted on The Boys coming back in. So kindly Tracey the nurse, allowed all four of them to be in there together with him. This was a special time for them all and they went in there laughing and smiling and their normal banter began – which is just what Lucas wanted.

I went home with Alisha later in the night while Les stayed with Lucas. Les made me promise that I would keep the routine going for Alisha's sake, so she had some normality. I was exhausted from the day's events, and was strangely *able* to sleep, as I knew Les was with Lucas.

The following morning when I called Les to hear about Lucas' condition, he told me his chest had been hurting a fair bit overnight. I had made up my mind then that I would be staying overnight that night and told Alisha to pack a bag as well, in preparation, should she need to go home with someone else in the evening.

ICU had been running various tests on him overnight and Dr Tom and the ICU consultant came into his room to tell us of their findings. We were basically told that his heart failure was progressing rapidly and it looked like it would be just days now instead of weeks! This was devastating news. We discussed as a family that we would not leave the hospital now, so we could be with him round the clock, that brought very *slight* comfort to Lucas.

Our families were back in the morning before we could let them know how dire things had become. I spoke to the ICU staff and told them we would have a lot of people coming in now and had their permission to use their interview room as a base where everyone could congregate. They all crammed into the room, taking it in turns visiting Lucas.

Every now and again Les and I would have a quick break from Lucas' room while someone else sat with him and when I went into the interview room, Jacqui had brought a variety of food for everyone. It was actually a heart-warming atmosphere (almost party-like), as there was laughter from the kids and everyone chatting, which was a welcome relief for me. Each time I went in there, more food would appear! Alex had bought burgers and drinks for everyone one time and despite all that was going on, the vibe was fairly upbeat.

Then the doctors all returned, this was not good. They advised us sadly that it was now looking hour to hour! I was sitting down, but vividly remember my head spinning as I simultaneously felt like I was outside of my body. This crushed us all, but I remained as positive as possible and prayed for some divine intervention. I just kept remembering them saying they had not seen this before in a cancer patient, where the heart, kidneys and lungs were all failing.

My prayers needed to be escalated, so I asked my mum, dad and Faith to come to the hospital's chapel with me. I prayed as hard as I could, begging for my son to be saved from this terrible fate. Such a good person didn't deserve this, surely God could see that. Not wanting to be away from Lucas for long, I left the three of them there, faithfully praying the Rosary together and for a miracle from God.

I think because we had been with Lucas day in and day out, Les and I hadn't noticed that his skin was an almost grey/green colour and his breathing was getting harder too. Our parents arranged a priest to visit Lucas and gave him his Last Rites blessing and even kissed him on his head. Sister Marie from the chapel who had often visited Lucas came also and she brought our religious parents some comfort in their despair. As confronting as this was, whoever from our immediate family was around at the time, were all permitted to come into the room and gather round his bed for this.

The support from our family and friends was incredible and kept us somewhat strong. They had remained at the hospital the whole day and into the night too. By evening more of Lucas' friends had arrived and gathered in the 'grungy' family room, as there were quite a few of them and they wouldn't fit in the interview room where family was gathered.

Declan's parents, Paula and Frank rang to let me know that Declan was on a flight from Kalgoorlie (where he was working) to Perth to see Lucas. I had to notify the nurses about Declan arriving, as during this time ICU went into lockdown. There was an emergency (which I had witnessed previously in ICU) which needed isolation and they needed to seal the doors to prevent infection, as a child was being operated on inside. Nobody was allowed in or out of ICU for one and a half hours. Some of our family and friends stayed, while others left to go home for a short break, it had been a tough couple of days.

Lucas was allowed to have all The Boys and India in his room with him. Les, Alisha and I didn't want to leave and there was not much space left in his tiny room, so Tracey opened a side door which led to another room where the three of us waited. This gave the kids some privacy, whilst the friends spent what was to be their last time together with him. Still lots of laughter coming from them all!

Declan finally arrived and Tracey ushered him through to Lucas. She decided that the other kids should leave for a while and let Declan have some time with his mate. They headed out into the family room again and were met in the meantime by Lucas' other friends, Desiree and her mum Barbara, along with Ciara and her parents Carmen and Duane, Paula, Declan's mum was waiting there too. Les and I had taken a break and were comforted by these friends of ours that had come down to the hospital.

Everyone started to congregate in the family room which was now filled with Lucas' friends, our friends and family. It was only at this time I was told, that my dad (who has early stages of dementia) had to have it explained to him, what was going on with Lucas and became very upset, as he hadn't really understood it up to that point.

There was an odd estranged couple in the family room, whose child was also in ICU. Every so often they would break into arguments, hurling insults loudly at each other across the room, for everyone to see and hear. The mother sitting on the floor, outside the family room and the father sitting *in* the family room, alongside our family and friends. When Faith walked into the room later, she gave everyone a kiss and kissed him too, as she thought he was just one of our friends that had gathered. It was only after someone asked why she kissed him she realised he wasn't with our crowd! This was quite hysterical at the time and lifted the mood temporarily.

Les and I had both made the decision to stay with Lucas overnight in his room, so the nurses kindly found an extra recliner chair, so we could at least be a little comfortable. Alisha didn't want to leave, nor did Tash so they were with Lucas' friends in the family room. The ICU staff had given us a room on the same floor in a nearby ward with a bed and couch in it, that Alisha, Tash and Declan later used.

CHAPTER FIFTEEN

18 Forever

As midnight rolled around, Les and I reluctantly wished Lucas Happy 18th Birthday. I cannot describe the misery of this situation. As I would come to know later from Ricky, all Lucas wanted for his 18th was to not be in any more pain. Alisha burst through his door and said "Lucas, it's your birthday, you can go to nightclubs now!" and he smiled. The three of us sang Happy Birthday to him as we had done so many times before. At the end of it, I said "Would you like some weed now?" An 'inside joke' for us and he smiled and shook his head to say yes! My son, always up for a laugh!

I offered him one of the cupcakes that Bec had baked for him, but knew that he couldn't eat it. Just a couple of days earlier Chloe and some of the other nurses were asking him what he would like to do for his birthday and they would try and arrange it. How drastically things had changed since then.

Alisha had considerately brought in with her that morning, a gorgeous photo of Lucas and herself and placed it where he could see it. She wanted to encourage him along and remind him of their loving bond, it was the only thing she felt she could do.

He was struggling more with his breathing now and was also getting extremely hot and was sweating (his heart working so hard, like he was running a marathon). One of the nurses organised a desk fan and placed it in front of him, next to the photo, to try and keep him cool, in addition to Les wiping him down frequently. The nurses also turned his oxygen up to the maximum level and gave him as much pain relief as was possible.

Alisha went back to the family room as Lucas just wanted to try and sleep now. As much as he craved sleep, his mind was racing and he was becoming very frustrated and eventually asked for something to help him sleep. This didn't seem to be effective and he was given more, but it wasn't much better.

As I left his room around 2.30am to get our coffees from the family room, to my surprise all the kids and Barbara, were still there. After I tried to convince them to go home, they told me they weren't going anywhere and were staying the night. The only thing I could do for them was take them some blankets, which they happily covered themselves with and sprawled out everywhere. Tash took a photo of this and sent it to me, this was precious.

Everyone was exhausted by this point and I managed to finally get Alisha, Tash and Declan to go rest in the room we had been given. Alisha made me promise that I would let her know if anything happened to Lucas. When I went back to his room I was so happy that I had the chance to show him that precious photo and said "Look Lucas, all your friends are still here." This made him smile, he was comforted by that thought and finally closed his eyes to sleep. Tash texted me saying that Alisha really wanted to be there if anything happened, which I agreed with.

About 3am things took a turn for the worse. I rang Tash and told her to bring Alisha in and Les also asked Tash if she'd like to come in too, which she thankfully did (Tash and Lucas had always been like siblings). Tash immediately went to Les and held onto him, while I held Alisha who was very upset. Seeing how distressed we were, Tash bravely took turns in comforting each one of us, despite what she herself would have been going through. This selfless act of love and kindness is something Les, Alisha and myself will always remember.

Lucas' breathing became very laboured, (something I had never seen before, but will remain etched in my memory forever). His heart rate was changing rapidly, as I kept an eye on his multiple monitor screens. Not wanting to become upset in front of him, we could no longer hold back our tears and immeasurable sadness. It was truly awful, as he had wires connected everywhere to his body and we couldn't even hold him or hug him properly. The best we could do was hold a *part* of him that was free from wires - hands, legs, head.

Then we had to say the most tormenting words a parent can say to their child, "It's ok, you need to let go now son." I could not believe those words were coming out of my mouth! But he just couldn't suffer anymore, it was too much for him to bear. I had to ask Alisha to tell him to let go as well, which she didn't understand at the time. Les also said to him "Say hi to Poppie for me when you see him." That really upset me, not because of *what* he said, but that it made it all so real. I just could not believe this was actually happening, and to my son. All I could say through my tears was "My precious baby boy" as I leaned over kissing him with one arm around his head and the other holding onto his hand.

He took his last struggled breath and he was gone. It was 3.30am. It happened so quickly and it didn't seem real. Although we'd all seen what had happened, we were left in shock and disbelief as it looked as though he was just sleeping. I wiped his mouth for the last time. The sharpness of sorrow piercing immediately through our shattered hearts. For Lucas though, he was now in peace, no more struggling, no more pain, no more worrying anymore.

Immediately after this happened Alisha had a massive hypoglycaemic episode (drop in blood sugar). I needed to take care of her, I knew, but I could not believe Lucas was gone. I sat her down and poured out her glucose drink, while Gill and Tracey, the nurses, ran around frantically to find her some food.

The nurses all hugged us and gave us their condolences. I watched as Tracey made sure all the wires and attachments were removed from Lucas and covered the main part of his body with a fresh sheet, mindful that the other kids there would probably never have seen anything like this before either and would be very distressed.

After some time we left his room, which was so hard for us. Les went to tell the kids in the family room and then courageously made the sad phone-calls to notify family, before heading outside the hospital to be alone briefly. I just couldn't face anyone at that moment and I guided Alisha and Tash back to their room. We didn't really talk very much, but it was comforting being together. I needed to lie down, so after a short while they left me lying on the couch and went back to join the others.

All I could think about was how a god could have let this happen to him. Where was the divine intervention? Where was the miracle that so many people had prayed for and had masses offered for? How, after everything Lucas had been through, even learning to walk again, had it come to this? I must have been in a state of shock, as I couldn't cry anymore at that point.

I closed my eyes for about 15 minutes and somehow managed to shut everything out. Alisha and Tash came back in and we packed their things and headed together to the family room. As more family and friends came in to the hospital, everyone had been allowed to go into his room and pay their respects whilst I was gone. Christabelle, Alex, Belinda, Faith, Jacqui and Paula were among the first to come back to the hospital to see Lucas and comfort us. This was incredibly hard for both them and ourselves, but we were grateful they were with us. Not long after, Pete brought Jaida and Liam in, which would have been so difficult for the kids to comprehend, but such a comfort for us and Alisha especially.

I went back in to see Lucas one last time, I just wanted to remember how it felt to hold his hand, now that I would no longer be able to hold it and touch his beautiful soft cheeks. I hadn't even realised that his body had already started to turn cold until Alisha spoke about it afterwards.

The Boys had messaged Lennon and he came down to the hospital, but we missed him. He was there for the kids though and has told me since, that they looked at him, like they were in Year 7 again and were desperate for comfort, which he definitely would've provided.

We finally left the hospital and walked to our cars. I was quite hysterical now, as I think all the emotion I had been holding back and not wanting to show in front of Lucas came flooding out. Belinda and Barbara guided me through the carpark. I was such a mess, as I thought about how I was leaving Lucas behind.

Alex drove my car as I was unable to and I went home with Les and Alisha. I just remember being on the freeway, it must have been about 5.30am by this time and other people were going about their business on their way to work, as the daily bustle of traffic had begun. It was an odd feeling knowing that none of these people were aware of what had just happened to my son and their lives were just going on as normal. Eventually after sobbing so much, I fell asleep the rest of the way until we got home. Then the real feeling of emptiness started to engulf me.

Our families came over that afternoon/early evening. Alex had organised this with everyone at the hospital before we left. At first, I couldn't bear the thought of this, but I was so grateful that he and

Christabelle took charge of it. For once I thankfully accepted the help of family while I just sat there. Bryan, my brother, had the job of fixing multiple gin and tonics to calm my wretched nerves. Frank and Paula had cooked and brought over so many different curries for everyone to share. We had so much left over that it fed us for the next couple of days. It was comforting being surrounded by our closest family members at this time.

After dinner we all gathered around and raised our glasses and a Happy 18th Birthday cheer to Lucas, it was bittersweet, but we still wanted to acknowledge it for our son's sake. Les and Declan both gave a very emotional speech. I had imagined Lucas' 18th for months now, being held in our new home, with family and friends, but not in this terrible way, in which he was not even present (physically anyway). He would remain 18 forever in my heart.

CHAPTER SIXTEEN

Lost Days

We had many lost days in the week between Lucas' passing and his funeral. We were devastated and heart broken, but we were so busy with funeral preparations and people dropping in to see us, it made the time a little more bearable, just to know that we weren't alone. We received so many phone-calls, messages, flowers, cards, candles, photo frames, plants, ornaments, trinkets, food, and numerous other gifts of support. I have never really understood, how people say they get strength from others until this happened to me and I will always remain grateful to everyone that has helped us in all sorts of meaningful ways and been there for us when we needed it most.

Lucas' funeral was an amazing occasion. We didn't have a church mass as he wouldn't have wanted that. We chose a simple service at a bright, airy and large chapel at Fremantle Cemetary. Les, Declan and The Boys were his pallbearers. When Les had asked The Boys if they would be Lucas' pallbearers, Ricky said "They would be honoured to carry Lucas, as he had always carried them."

We were in awe of the sheer number of people that had gathered to pay their respects to our son. And we were later told by the funeral directors, that they ran out of guest cards to give people, of which they had four hundred. They estimated there were about five to six hundred people there. Sarah and Bev (oncology nurses), Anne and other hospital staff were present. Also Brad (Paige's dad) and Couper with his mum Kierstyn (all from the hospital) had also come in support. Lucas' boss Peter and his wife Sue were there also. Along with some of Lucas' Yidarra and Corpus school teachers and staff members. After the service the condolences were overwhelming, but we were grateful to stand there greeting all these thoughtful people. We were honoured that Lucas had touched so many people's lives and we were truly blessed to have that support and love.

We had the wake back at our home with family and friends. The Boys together with Lennon had made a 'Happy 18th Lucas' sign and photo's which they pinned onto his pinup board in his room. All of them sat up in Lucas' room for a long time. Lennon also brought helium balloons and all the kids that were there went out into the front yard and released them, which was beautiful to watch.

Les had, and rightly so, a fair bit to drink that night and proceeded to give Lucas' friends 'life advice', which I'm sure Lucas would have been cringing at the thought of! He showed them how to smoke cigars and drank with them too. The vibe was uplifting, rather than sombre, which was lovely. It was great to hear laughter and chatter amongst everyone, honouring Lucas in a happy way. The love and support we received that day from our loving family and dear friends will be cherished in our hearts forever.

CHAPTER SEVENTEEN

Feelings

I remember so clearly after the immense loss of my son, driving numerous times to go somewhere and not realising how I'd gotten from one place to another (just being on auto-pilot). But I honestly could not control my mind from wandering whilst I was driving, leading to the perpetual question that I continue to ask – "Why?"

The elusive answer still escapes me now, but through desperation I would cry, which would inevitably lead to me screaming out loud in the car. It was both tragic and cathartic at the same time and I did this quite often in the beginning of my grief process.

Another part of my own process and the feelings it brought about for me, was to go back into the hospital and thank both the ICU staff and the oncology ward staff. I knew from the start that I had to do this, it just seemed right in my mind to show my gratitude for the care they had taken of our son.

The day I chose to do this was after my first counselling session at Redkite. I was feeling courageous and somewhat relieved after the session and just turned my car in the direction of the hospital and told myself "You can do this!"

Even parking in the familiar hospital carpark was hard. When I walked through the hospital doors I felt my heart beating rapidly, but I just sucked it up, as that was nothing in comparison to what Lucas went through. I went straight up to the ICU floor. As I needed to 'buzz in' when I reached the ICU doors, I wasn't sure what I was going to say. I was used to saying "I'm here to see Lucas" and they'd see me on the camera and let me through, but what did I say this time? To my good fortune a friendly nurse recognised me and welcomed me into the ward.

Another stroke of luck, was that many of the ICU nurses that had looked after Lucas were there at that time and I had the opportunity to thank them personally, as they huddled around me crying and hugging me. Amazing how over such a short period of time, the affection that one person could draw was displayed in such a meaningful way. It was bitter sweet to see them again and even though they told me I was a brave lady, I didn't feel brave, it was simply a matter of showing my appreciation for their hard work and kindness to our son and family.

Then I did the same thing in the oncology ward, but wasn't so lucky this time, as many of the staff that I had wanted to see were not there at the time, but I passed on my thanks regardless. This was equally tough as I had walked these corridors so many times over the months, but this time not to see Lucas.

A few weeks later I met with Anne and Shani (the hospital teachers) after they'd finished work for the day. We laughed, became teary and drank a toast to Lucas together!

I noticed a sense of relief driving home from there that day.

CHAPTER EIGHTEEN

Extraordinary

The following are extraordinary things that have happened since Lucas has been gone.

Peter and India went to see Lennon after school had finished the day Lucas passed, as they needed to talk about things with him. India told Lennon that the class he currently teaches in was Lucas' old Year 6 classroom at Yidarra!

Also that evening, The Boys had met at Corpus (where they had graduated only a few months earlier) and gathered with some of their friends in their old hangout spot by the pond. They took a birthday cake and sang happy birthday to Lucas and then oddly only one of the candles blew out by itself!

The morning after Lucas passed, we were woken early by the piercing sound of an alarm. I jumped out of bed as I thought it was the house alarm, but discovered that it was coming from one of our fire detector alarms. We had moved in to our newly built home only three weeks prior and the fire alarms were 'hard wired', so they should not have alarmed, for no reason, like battery operated alarms may. After what felt like a very long time and a phone-call to the electrician who fitted them, Les thought maybe he would just try to change the backup batteries (in order to try something whilst waiting for the electrician). It worked, the alarm stopped. Les said it was like Lucas was sending him a sign to get up and get on with it!

In the same morning, as I had my shower, I looked twice to notice a pattern on the tiled shower floor. The bubbles from the body wash made a large unmistakably perfect love-heart!

I had a strange fleeting thought that Lucas may have taken the form of a seagull now. As we live near the beach there are plenty of them around, so I dismissed the thought and never mentioned it to anyone, for fear of being thought of as crazy. Les was working in the garage with the garage door open and called me to come see this unusually tame seagull. Alisha and I both went outside and the seagull didn't fly away, it was just happily walking around our cars. Les even walked up close to it and it was not fussed. We fed it some bread and took pictures of it too. Obviously by then I had told Les and Alisha what I had thought about the seagull.

After he passed, Alisha had started wearing Lucas t-shirts (and socks in winter), to bed. She still wears a different t-shirt each night. Belinda had written to Mitchell Coombes a well known psychic, who has a column in the Woman's Day magazine. She wanted to ask him why it was her nephew's time to pass. She was chosen to have a psychic reading and we were both present on the day the reading occurred.

During the reading he had 'picked up' that someone was wearing Lucas' t-shirts and socks! He also knew that I placed in his casket, something from Lucas' childhood, that was made by him and it had to do with hands and hearts. I placed a magnet Lucas made for me in his suit pocket on the day of his viewing. It was a macaroni magnet that he made in Kindy, that read 'Mothers hold their children's hands a while, but hold their hearts forever'. Nobody but Les and Alisha knew that I had done this and Belinda was stunned to hear about this after the reading. There were many other accurate things Mitchell mentioned and in February 2018 part of this reading was published in the magazine.

A few weeks after Lucas passed I received a call from the Make a Wish Foundation. They were ringing to say everything had been approved and they could send us on the luxury fishing charter up north. I had to stop the girl from talking and gave her the news. She felt so bad (and so did I), as I'm pretty sure she had started crying on the other end of the phone.

In July 2017 we met with Dr Tom from oncology for his empathetic medical debrief regarding Lucas. As we were driving to the meeting, looking for a parking spot, one of Lucas' favourite songs by Childish Gambino came on the radio right as we drove past the hospital!

During the year, Lennon rang to tell me that one of Lucas' old, still labelled, Yidarra school jumpers had turned up as a spare jumper in the classroom, where Lennon now teaches – Lucas' old Year 6 classroom!

The Boys visit us regularly. On one occasion we met them for dinner at Nando's. The night before we met, I had a very brief dream of Lucas, the first I had of him since he'd passed. He was with The Boys and they were going to Kings Park by Uber. Peter asked me if he could borrow our cutlery and chopsticks before they left our house. Later in the dream I was in the back passenger seat of a car Alisha was driving and Lucas yelled out to me "Hey Uber" and The Boys all started doing the same. I put my window down and showed him a bottle of washing detergent and said "Look what I have to do" and laughed. I have no idea what this random dream is and can make no sense of it! But when we caught up with The Boys for dinner at Nando's, they mentioned to us that the previous night they all went up to Kings Park together!

Recently I was gazing out the window looking into the night sky before I closed the blinds, as I do every night. I whispered quietly "Lucas if you can hear me give me a sign". A star lit up so brightly and then vanished and then a few seconds later did the same thing and then it was gone! This made me smile.

AFTERWORD

Change

I like to think that now Lucas is somewhere like heaven, enjoying his days fishing with his Poppie, or thinking of ways to prank God with his humour and his nights with others up there, partying to music with Tupac, Prince and Elvis.

I feel grateful and honoured to have had a teacher as rich as Lucas in my life, who continues to bring me strength, inspiration and appreciation of life. In his name I will live by sharing stories, laughing lots (always) and enjoying it all while I have the opportunity.

Change is part of the new life for Les, Alisha and myself, but Lucas' loving and cherished memory will be kept safe in our hearts forever. And I take comfort in knowing that we have our very own special guardian angel to watch over us always.

ACKNOWLEDGEMENTS

I am so grateful for so many things. Firstly, for the gift of my precious son Lucas into my life, who has taught me so many beautiful things and left me with such wonderful memories to cherish forever. My amazing husband Les, for his continual love, shared tears and support during this, the hardest time of our lives. My wonderful daughter Alisha who has shown amazing strength after dealing with this immense loss herself. For giving me some form of focus during these trying times and her ability to keep a smile on my face (most of the time!)

My parents Joan and Ken, for their love and support of us during this time and always. Les' parents Faith and Bunny, for their acceptance and love for their grandchildren. And the ongoing support of our immediate families which has been invaluable.

CONNORS FAMILY

Christabelle and Tash, who have been a constant support for Alisha and myself, especially when Les was working away. Tash, bringing me flowers at every month's end and Christabelle, remembering to message me at that time too, just a tiny glimpse of their thoughtfulness.

Belinda and Darren, who unfailingly came to the hospital and were by Lucas' side for a chat and encouragement and have helped me immensely throughout also.

Jacqui, who through her own understanding and empathy has shared many tears with me.

Our close group of beautiful friends, who have been unbelievably caring and supportive of us and continue to be. Vanessa & Alan, Tiala & Mike, Tania, Nigel, Rachel & Mark, Alvin, Mirella, Rob & Rod. Vanessa, who was there for me in my darkest hours, I will always treasure your friendship and thank you also for your help with reading through this. The girls for continuing to check on me and help keeping me sane and smiling. Nigel, who always shares his insight and wit with us. Alvin who gave me the best advice in seeking help to move forward (let's not let this go to your head Alvin!) And Rachel who suggested to take some time for myself.

My wonderful group of Western Power girls, your laughter, tears and love have given me strength and kept me grounded (Vanessa, Steph, Vicki J, Sharoyn, Batch, Debbie, Tanya, Sue, Bona & Vicki R). Lee the 'biscuit lady', thank you for our chats and supply of shortbread.

Barbara and Carmen helping me through conversation and coffee.

The Boys (Peter, Ricky, James and Joseph) thank you for being such wonderful friends to Lucas. Together with India, you all popping round and visiting us has been a great comfort and support to us and in particular Alisha.

Declan, Paula, Frank and your girls, your friendship is so generous (and your food unbelievable!)

Lennon for being a wonderfully inspirational teacher and friend to both Lucas and our family. The world would be a much kinder place if we have more teachers like you in it.

Anne and Shani for being fantastic hospital support for me at a crazy time. And Shani who provided her feedback on my book too. Author AJ Betts who I met at the hospital and inspired me to keep writing. Peter Kerwin from the hospital for listening to me.

Julia from Chakra Angel for her encouragement, which led me to using Lucas' desk while I wrote this.

The ladies from Redkite, Sasha and Jo who have helped me through their compassion.

Maureen from Solaris Cancer Centre who has helped me work through so much, empowered me to become stronger and who kindly gave me her thoughts on my writing. Julie, Richie and all the other lovely people at Solaris.

Finally, thank you to all who have helped Les, Alisha and myself in any way through the most difficult time we will ever face, we are so truly grateful.

ABOUT THE AUTHOR

Through her everchanging face of motherhood, Suz Connors uses what she knows best, humour and authenticity, to deliver her passion to encourage others to live a grateful life. With a loving heart and positive mind she is empowered to tell her son's inspirational story.

Printed in the United States
By Bookmasters